DRUMS IN MY EARS

Benny Green

Drums in my ears

Jazz in our Time

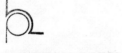

HORIZON PRESS   NEW YORK

First published in the United States in 1973 by Horizon Press

Copyright © 1973 by Benny Green

Library of Congress Catalog Card No. 72 96386

ISBN 0 8180 1209 9

735270

Printed in Great Britain by
Bristol Typesetting Company Limited
Bristol

To Kenneth Tynan

The author and publisher wish to thank *The Guardian,* *New Society,* the *Observer,* *Punch* and *Queen* for permission to print extracts from their journals.

CONTENTS

Introduction

I was indeed born with drums in my ears, more or less. My first connections with jazz were established on December 9, 1927, when, by performing the act of being born, I acquired among other things a saxophone-playing father. Under his benign tutelage I blew a soprano saxophone for the first time in November, 1941, and blew it for the first time before an audience not composed exclusively of blood relatives in February, 1943. As my repertoire at the time consisted in its entirety of an old jazz standard called 'Whispering' and a tearjerker of the period called 'Whispering Grass', I had no alternative but to keep repeating this oddly *sotto voce* repertoire throughout the evening, but nobody seemed to notice, least of all the dancers, too preoccupied as usual with the fluctuations of their own private dramas to hear the music.

The occasion was an obscure club dance in a church hall somewhere at the back of Marble Arch and was an event of the deepest possible significance for me for two reasons. First, it was my initiation into the terrifying rite of performing before people who, having paid for admission, consider themselves to be finer judges of music than the musicians, who have not only not paid for admission, but have actually turned up expecting to be paid for it; second, it planted in my mind, numbed though it was by a lack of worldliness approaching complete imbecility, the tiny seed of a suspicion destined not to flower for many years yet, that perhaps not all those who strove for technical mastery over an instrument were moved by purely aesthetic motives. Something about the way the drummer kept grumbling about his fee, allied to the persistence with which his friend, the clarinettist, kept checking the findings of the clock on the facing wall with those of his wrist-watch, suggested as much to me. The truth of these suspicions, that there might just conceivably be such a thing as a musician who disliked music, or had no real interest in its welfare, was confirmed long after, when I discovered that, of the members of that very first band, one had become a recording executive and the other a successful music publisher.

I, on the other hand, was an apprentice of palpitating sincerity, a fanatic with the lily of aesthetic endeavour clutched so firmly between my teeth that very often there was no room there for my saxophone mouthpiece. This proved true on a Saturday night in June, 1947, when, booked to appear for the first time with a band whose members included two real professionals, I was so disturbed by the prospect of my coming ordeal that I was unable to get any sleep the night before, and finally turned up for the engagement minus the mouthpiece of my instrument. The occasion was a dance at the Wilkinson Sword Factory in Acton and there was nothing for me to do but leave my colleagues to struggle on without me, while I turned round and went back by public transport to my home in Euston, where I found my mouthpiece in the top drawer of the bureau, wrapped lovingly in a sheet of clean muslin in which condition I was in the habit of leaving it after each day's practice. Grabbing it, I travelled back to Acton, where I arrived just in time to play two choruses of 'Pennies From Heaven' and one of the National Anthem before returning once more to Euston. For this sustained feat of mobility the bandleader paid me the sum of thirty-two shillings, which, representing as it did an increase of nearly 1,300 per cent on my Marble Arch church hall début, left me contented enough.

The first time I played with a band and was then invited to come back and play with it again was on January 1, 1949, and the occasion when, comprising one seventh of a fully professional orchestra, presumably I became fully professional myself, occurred exactly six months later, on July 1, 1949. It was on an afternoon during this engagement that I recognised among the crowd of eight or ten people which comprised our average tea-dance attendance, the face of Ronnie Scott, a musician I hero-worshipped so violently at the time that from the moment I spotted him I found myself unable to produce enough saliva to produce a sound from my instrument, and was therefore reduced to the ignominy of pretending to tinker with the mechanism of my saxophone, of whose structure and workings I had, of course, not the remotest conception.

Two years later I was hired to play for the first time in an orchestra not unknown to the general public, and a year later I became a member of a quintet led by the same Ronnie Scott. It was at this time, in December, 1952, that a musical performance of mine was analysed in print for the first time ('. . . although a newcomer to these columns . . . already a most accomplished performer . . .'), although by this time, having already seen myself in print twice in the musical press, I was less inclined to take the event with quite the same degree of seriousness I might have done a year or two earlier.

In the spring of 1955 I began contributing a weekly column to one of the musical papers, on any subject I pleased, although there was an unspoken agreement between the editor and myself that I must not poach on the preserves of the 'serious' reviewers on the staff, it being generally thought at that time that a practical knowledge of making jazz was an insuperable barrier to writing about it coherently. In 1957 the editorship of this paper changed hands, which meant that all the new editor's journalistic friends replaced all the old editor's journalistic friends, including myself. A month later I joined a rival musical weekly, where I soon drifted into the duties of film, jazz, drama and literary reviewer and Elian essayist, juggling with so many *noms de plume* that there were some weeks when the column under my own name consisted in its entirety of bitter debate with other aspects of my splintered journalistic self.

Some time after I began my weekly pieces, but before I changed papers, I met Kenneth Tynan. All I can remember of this meeting is that it occurred in an all-night jazz club in Lisle Street, and that Tynan's début as the *Observer* drama critic was due in a few hours' time. Two years later he suddenly phoned to ask me if I would be interested in applying for the job of jazz critic on his paper, explaining to me that I should submit a few published pieces for scrutiny. At that time, although still a working jazz musician, with the Dizzy Reece Quintet, I happened to be involved in a very brief but very exotic episode as the figurehead of an enterprise called 'Jazz City', an institution which must surely have established some kind of record for the amazing rapidity of its decline from opulence to utter pauperdom, there being 1,050 paying customers at our opening Saturday night, and twelve at our closing one six weeks later. (On our second night, having booked John Dankworth's Orchestra, we found ourselves so flooded with customers that at one point, while helping a

11

relative of mine to sneak in for nothing through the back entrance, I was locked out of the building, and had the piquant experience of bunking into my own club.)

Tynan agreed to come down to 'Jazz City' one Saturday night to collect my literary samples, and although I have no idea what it was I gave him to read, I do recall quite distinctly that in spite of strict orders to my partners in the box-office that Tynan, being on an errand of mercy so to speak, should be allowed in free, he and his friends were obliged to pay 8/6 a head for the privilege of collecting a few of my press cuttings. Nevertheless some months later I joined the *Observer*.

I am unable to account for any of the incidents in this odd tale, least of all why Tynan, who hardly knew me, and had almost certainly never read me, should have taken so much trouble to alter the course of my life, which he did beyond any question, in the most benign sense.

On the day my first review appeared, on the Beaulieu Jazz Festival, August Bank Holiday, 1958, jazz was in several respects still a comparatively innocent music. It is true that Miles Davis was already committed to the experiments involving the abandonment of the hitherto obligatory frame of harmonic progression from discord to resolution, true also that names like Sonny Rollins and John Coltrane were familiar to all students of the music. On the other hand, both Louis Armstrong and Duke Ellington were still young enough to have produced some of their finest work only a year or two before, Armstrong with 'Satch Plays Fats', Ellington with his Shakespearean vignettes, 'Such Sweet Thunder'. Players like Dizzy Gillespie and Jay Jay Johnson, Cannonball Adderley and Oscar Peterson were still regarded as extreme moderns, and the degree of our innocence may be gauged from the fact that only a year previously, in New York in 1957, Ronnie Scott had advised me to come and see 'the greatest saxophonist in the world', Sonny Stitt, who was appearing across the river in Newark, and that after taking Scott's advice, I saw no reason to argue with his description.

Many of the dominant figures of the pre-war Swing Age were still not only alive but kicking. Lester Young and Billie Holiday, Coleman Hawkins and Johnny Hodges, Sidney Bechet and Billy Strayhorn, Jack Teagarden and Henry Allen – none of these had qualified yet for memorial albums. Art Tatum and Clifford Brown had been dead only two years, Charlie Parker three, Django Reinhardt five. As for the shocking suggestion, accepted in more recent times without the batting of an eye, that jazz might after all turn out to be a finite art, almost nobody had considered the possibility. In 1958 jazz was just emerging from the disastrous internecine wars caused by the Bebop revolution of the mid-1940s, or rather by critical reaction to it. Only now was the heat beginning to go out of the argument. People still listened, and wrote, and thought, however, in terms of the rigid compartments of jazz so obligingly but so misleadingly supplied by critics. Like Caesar's Gaul or the old Victorian novel, jazz was divided into three parts, Traditional, Mainstream and Modern, although as there was nobody who could define any of these terms to anybody else's satisfaction, certain difficulties presented themselves. There was Duke Ellington, for instance. He had recorded 'Black and Tan Fantasy' in 1927. 'Take the "A" Train' in 1940, 'Star-Crossed Lovers' in 1957, so presumably he must be Traditional, Mainstream and Modern at the same time. And a player like, say, Illinois Jacquet although far more derivative than, say, Bix Beiderbecke, must be considered the more modern of the two simply because Bix died in 1931, when Jacquet was only nine years old.

The truth was that Modernism in jazz, and indeed in everything else, was not a style but an attitude, and it was an attitude discernible not only in the reaction of each musician to the harmonic conventions of his era, but in the precise date on which he may have attempted some departure from those conventions. In other arts this presented no difficulty. For a painter to pursue Impressionism in 1958 would require merely a hero-worship of Monet. To have adopted the identical method in 1758 would demand extremes of courage and originality amounting to genius. The problem was that in jazz, where the rate of evolution was so hysterical that in fifty years it had moved from Primitivism to Sentimental Revivalism, the displacement of a year, or even of six months, might mean all the difference between a stroke of true originality and one of mere ingenious imitation. It seemed to me unfair that a player like Lester Young, whose brilliant exposition of the use of the chord of the minor sixth had been delivered in 'Dickie's Dream' as early as 1937, should be deprived of the credit simply because within a year there were a dozen disciples doing the same thing.

One of the most remarkable things about the jazz fraternity is the speed with which it can assimilate new findings. Indeed this speed is so remarkable that it has always been taken for granted as a fact of life, instead of for the phenomenon it really is. As a working musician I had already seen, and occasionally participated in, the process by which some new phrase arrived on an American recording, was then dissected, examined and reassembled, and finally reproduced in the local jazz clubs, not by one or two players, but by every musician living the jazz life at the time. And so it was in the American jazz world only more so. A performance like Charlie Teagarden's with the Venuti-Lang All Stars in 1932 would always be moving and beautiful; had it been achieved without foreknowledge of Beiderbecke, then Teagarden would have been one of the great figures of jazz history instead of a charming and talented background character. Similarly, the incandescence of Sonny Stitt which so excited Scott and myself in Newark, 1957, would perhaps have unhinged us altogether had we not been at least partly insulated against the effects of such passionate dexterity by knowledge over the previous ten years of Charlie Parker. My problem was, how to codify the harmonic life of such musicians without reducing the actual writing, at least so far as the layman was concerned, to technical gibberish.

One other factor was of extreme importance in Britain in 1958. Only two years before, a crude and imperceptive union ban on visiting American jazz musicians had been lifted. This ban had obtained for twenty-five years, which meant that a whole generation of jazz fanciers had grown up who had literally never heard the real thing in the flesh. In 1958 we were still a little overwhelmed by imports, and the visits of Americans, steadily increasing in frequency as they declined in effect, comprised a large slice of every reviewer's life. There were thriving at this time two bloated reputations which I did my best to deflate, those of John Lewis and Dave Brubeck. Eventually they arrived within weeks of each other at the tail-end of 1959, and I suppose I was as relentless in my pursuit of them as they were in pursuit of British audiences. The 1972 reader may find it difficult to comprehend quite how vast the Modern Jazz Quartet and Brubeck bulked in 1958. It seemed to me that their exalted positions were not only false but usurped, for there were many jazz musicians more gifted than they whose neglect was as scandalous as it was pathetic. In time the reputations of both Lewis and Brubeck were to subside, particularly Brubeck's. Indeed, his almost total retirement from the jazz life, as sudden as it was gratifying, had so disastrous an effect on his reputation that he may be said to have performed the Byronic exercise backwards, by awaking one morning to find himself obscure.

The jazz life has changed beyond recognition since the day I first went to the Beaulieu Festival on Tynan's suggestion. As for my own, having begun it with the purchase of Frank Trumbauer's 'Singing the Blues', having continued it by playing the sedulous ape, first to Benny Goodman and then to Lester Young, having moved from the sentimental jollities of Jewish wedding repertoires in 1948 to the Chicago-style jollities of Freddie Randall's band in 1950 to the *avant garde* jollities of Ronnie Scott's band two years later, I had, by the time I began composing the pieces which follow, a great many axes to grind. I have been grinding them ever since, whenever the opportunity has presented itself, and sometimes even when it hasn't.

Benny Green

Heroes Ancient and Modern

BIX 1956
MAN AND MYTH

It is twenty-five years since Bix Beiderbecke, the baby-faced apotheosis of the jazz age, died of consumption and rather unkindly left us to the torrid speculations of writers determined to make every dead jazzman a tragic hero – for of all the tragic heroes who were ever deified in the name of jazz, Bix Beiderbecke has always been depicted as the most tragic and the most heroic.

The Beiderbecke myth was inevitable. The ingredients were too convenient to be ignored – the unlined face, the towering talent, the quixotic temperament, and the premature death juxtaposed with Capone's Empire.

Hero-worship was no less inflated than finance at the time, and when one recalls the elephantine bulk of the legends of the period – the Dempsey legend, the Babe Ruth legend, the Lindbergh legend – it is not surprising that even the jazz world romanticised its heroes, although at least in the case of Bix it romanticised the right one.

There was also that most potent factor of all, the shadow of consumption. Bix Beiderbecke is probably the most romanticised consumptive since Dumas *fils*' 'Lady of the Camellias'. Today it is difficult to listen to Bix without hearing the overtones of the legend, and quite impossible to extricate oneself completely from the morass of myth his name became bogged down in long ago.

I was one of the fortunate ones. I heard the music before I heard the legend, which was so unfamiliar to me I thought for a while the man's name was Bick Spiderbecke.

By the time I encountered Miss Dorothy Baker's shamelessly mawkish 'Young Man With A Horn', I was already insulated by the catholicity of personal experience as a musician from the farrago of nonsense which quickly gathered around his name after 1931 – the year he died in circumstances so obscured by silly legend that we have all been left with the uneasy feeling he has been peeping over our shoulders ever since.

Bix was the prototype of the string of threepenny library cardboard heroes whose 'bell-like tones float across the night' with monotonous inevitability, who die unloved, their genius thwarted. One recalls Miss Baker's arch introductory howler in endowing her hero with a musical capacity 'equal to say, Bach's', and Mr Goffin's frenzied portrait of a Bix with the wisps of destiny swirling across his brain.

On the cover of one of the Bix LPs is a representation of our hero, with that beatific face and the angelic demeanour which fit so snugly into the context of the legend. And what a legend!

Those quaint photos of the Wolverines with the panto-mime-backdrop landscapes painted on the bass drum, the stories of frozen applejack in mid-western winters, the commentators with their tight-lipped resolution to be charitable about the rumours of marijuana and their tidy homiletics on the clean life and how Bix's genius excuses the deviations, the hackneyed quotes from mimetic dilettantes who insult the memory of the man by imitating instead of trying to create.

There are at least half a dozen versions of Bix's arrival on the jazz scene and a dozen more of his end, and the idolator may take his choice. But what of those who desire to ignore the superstructure of fetishism and discover the musician underneath?

Bix was more unfortunate in his musical companions than any jazzman of comparable stature, for by no stretch of the critical imagination could it be claimed that the Bill Ranks and the Min Leibrooks and the Howdy Quicksells (impossible name!) were fit to swig from the same hip flask as Bix.

Of course there was Trumbauer who died the other day, twenty years too late to become a legend himself, but it is true to say that Bix rarely if ever recorded in worthy company, and one can only speculate on what might have been – had Bix not been surrounded by so many lame dogs.

There is no question that his gifts surpassed those of all his white contemporaries, most of whom are only remembered through the Bix association, and that taken in his context of place and time, his greatness and permanence as a classic are undisputed and indisputable.

When I listen to 'Singing the Blues' I am reminded of the

man who, when taken to see 'Hamlet' for the first time, said, 'Yes, but it's full of quotations.' The surviving Chicagoans continue their attempts to hammer into the ground the great beauty of the original, which becomes increasingly difficult to hear without recalling Bobby Hackett's scored band chorus and the more recent skeletal rattlings of Jimmy McPartland.

One listens now to the 1927 Trumbauer version with a curious tensed anticipation. The astonishing thing is that Bix's solo, despite the plunderings of Hackett and McPartland, still retains the pristine glory which has driven so many hacks to the metaphor of bell-chimes.

Hoagy Carmichael, that master-purveyor of whimsy, can recite anecdotes of Bix *ad nauseam*, and even the greenest tyro will have heard of the theory that 'Stardust' is Bixian improvisation slowed down and lyricised.

In 'Hear Me Talking To Ya', Carmichael, recalling Bix's last days, strikes a blend of sentiment and reverence in drawing a veil of mysticism about Bix— 'She didn't know who Bix was. Then I suddenly realised. I didn't either.'

Over that viscous literary stew 'Young Man with a Horn' it may perhaps be charitable to draw my own veil, though it must be admitted that the book is based on 'the music not the life of Bix Beiderbecke'. What Bix would have made of Rick Martin and Amy North and Smoke Jordan is yet another insoluble riddle.

As Hollywood's 'Young Man of Music' was a vulgarisation of a vulgarisation, no further reference need be made to it in an essay on Bix, except to say that Miss Baker was at least honest enough to kill her hero off, and that Hollywood wasn't.

After twenty-five years the fey figure of Bix has become a talisman of the era he dominated – an age of harmonic innocence in jazz and the tubercular flush on the complexion of the times so poignantly mirrored in 'The Great Gatsby' by Scott Fitzgerald, with his 'silver slippers shuffled in the dust to the Beale Street Blues'.

It is because of the peculiar emotional appeal of this background that many outsiders who know of Fitzgerald but not of jazz, rush upon Bix and symbolise him as all kinds of improbable things. A pity, because Bix was too gifted a musician to need the trappings of a legend to seduce the listener.

DUKE 1958

When Duke Ellington and his Orchestra open their tour at the Royal Festival Hall in London tonight, it will be the first time a British audience has sighted his group for twenty-five years. In 1933 Ellington conquered Britain from the Prince of Wales downwards and since then connoisseurs of jazz music have longed for his return, but Ellington's neurotic aversion from long-distance travel and the recently concluded cold war between the British and American Musicians' Unions have both combined to prevent it.

On that first triumphant visit Ellington was undisputed leader in his field; today, despite or perhaps because of his refusal to get mixed up in any of the coterie movements which periodically transform the rapidly evolving art of jazz, he still is. Two generations of popular entertainment have slipped by since he first began to make his orchestra sound typically Ellingtonian, and many of the names of his one-time contemporaries today evoke only faint nostalgia – Paul Whiteman, Ted Lewis, Jimmie Lunceford, Benny Goodman. But in his sixtieth year the Duke remains master of a profession not noted for the durability of its reputations.

The chief characteristic of the Ellington personality is excess. He is a prodigious worker and a man of gargantuan appetites. His physical frame is massive: the pouches under his eyes are the biggest in show business. He has written nearly 2,000 songs and earned over a million dollars. He wrote 'Solitude' during a twenty-minute break in a recording. He composed the 'Liberian Suite' because the Liberian Government commissioned him to do so. Despite his age, which is very advanced for a touring bandleader, he still goes on gruelling itineraries and pours out a flood of original music. His present band is very nearly the best he has ever mustered.

Ellington was born in Washingon, DC, in 1899, at about the time jazz was emerging from its pre-history into some kind of coherence. As a child he learned the piano from a woman who he has always insisted was called Mrs Klinkscale. By the time he was fifteen he had discovered the local kings of 'stride' piano and written his first composition.

A scholarship in commercial art almost got him away to a

false start, but the Duke discovered that in wartime Washington orchestras for local dances were eagerly sought after. Soon he found himself supplying bands all over the city. During these early days a few of the musicians who later became part of the great Ellington organisation drifted into his orbit, but it was not until 1927, after the inevitable move to New York, that real success began.

The Ellington band was working at the Kentucky Club one night when a band-booker-cum-lyricist called Irving Mills came in. Each man has recorded his impression of this first meeting. According to Ellington, 'We were playing "St Louis Blues" and he asked what it was. When I told him, he said it sure sounded nothing like it. So maybe that gave him ideas.' Mills recalls: 'I immediately recognised that I had encountered a great creative artist – the first American composer to catch in his music the true jazz spirit.'

The success story really dates from this time. Ellington moved to the Cotton Club, and by 1932 was making $60,000 a year, at which stage the fruits of victory began to pall. He got bored, and the cure turned out to be the first European tour. The French surrealist poet Blaise Cendrars wrote, 'Such music is not only a new art form, but a new reason for living.' Less hysterical was the reply of one of Ellington's musicians when he was asked by a French critic if his boss was a genius: 'He's a genius all right, but Jesus, how he eats.'

In 1935 the Duke's homespun faith in a benevolent Deity was shattered by the death of his mother. 'I wrote "Reminiscin' in Tempo" that year. It was one of my first ambitious things. It was written in a soliloquising mood. My mother's death was the greatest shock. I didn't do anything but brood. The music is representative of that. It begins with pleasant thoughts. Then something awful gets you down. Then you snap out of it and it ends affirmatively.'

Most Ellington connoisseurs will tell you that the band he led around the years 1939–41 was the best he ever had. No band in jazz history has quite matched its diversity of solo talent or its spirited cohesion. In those days the notorious Ellington desire for a peaceful life was still well in evidence. There were no spoken preambles between numbers. Often three or four musicians would saunter on stage in the middle of a performance.

Cynics say this is the real reason why musicians never leave Ellington; the boss is too easy-going. Whatever the reason, Ellington's band is unique in this constancy of its members. Two of the saxophonists at the Royal Festival Hall this evening, Johnny Hodges and Harry Carney, were with the Duke on his British tour twenty-five years ago. This is Carneys's thirty-second year as an Ellington side-man.

Even inside the jazz-world, the precise nature of Ellington's method is often woefully misunderstood. He is neither the archetypal pianist-dance-band-leader who plugs his own material, nor the ordinary kind of western composer. Ellington writes, not for woodwind, brass and rhythm, but for the individual members of his orchestra.

This is the essence of the Ellington method and the real reason why changes in his band are so rare. He has to have a stable group. Moreover, when changes do occur, Ellington shows uncanny judgement in introducing an apparently incongruous element and merging it into the authentic Ellington texture. Nobody who has ever worked for Ellington is ever quite the same musician again. His musical collaborator and assistant, pianist Billy Strayhorn, put the situation aptly when he said: 'Ellington plays the piano, but his real instrument is his band. Each member of his band is to him a distinctive tone, colour and set of emotions, which he mixes with others equally distinctive to produce a third thing, which I like to call the Ellington Effect.'

Ellington has the jazz musician's customary distrust of critics Yet he himself can be pretty profuse about his own work. Describing 'Harlem Air Shaft', he once said: 'So much goes on in a Harlem air shaft. You get the full essence . . . you hear fights, you smell dinner, you hear people making love. You hear intimate gossip floating down. You hear the radio. You see your neighbour's laundry . . . you smell coffee, a wonderful thing, is that smell. . . .'

This remembrance of things past is the key to the Ellingtonian aesthetic. One of his most characteristic sayings is: 'The memory of things gone is important to a jazz musician.' To Ellington, music is emotion recollected in something a little more animated than tranquillity; all his whimsical theme synopses contain this dominant streak of nostalgia.

Of 'Mood Indigo', one of his most ingenious and delicate pieces, he explains: 'Just a story about a little girl and a little boy. They are about eight and the girl loves the boy. They never speak it of course, but she just likes the way he wears his hat. Every day he comes to her house at a certain time and she sits in her window and waits. Then, one day he doesn't come. "Mood Indigo" just tells how she feels.'

Much of the material British audiences will hear is comparatively recent, like 'Such Sweet Thunder', the set of twelve Shakespearean vignettes the Ellington band first performed last year. It is questionable whether there is any affinity between Ellingtonian ideas and Elizabethan sensibilities – or even whether there is much real relationship between Shakespeare's Hamlet and the Duke's. What a work like this does do is suggest that Ellington is one of the most remarkably endowed composers of music alive today.

LESTER 1959
A MATTER OF DATES

The tenor saxophonist Lester Young presents one of the most awkward problems with which the contemporary critic has to contend. With Young, more than any other jazzman of the last twenty-five years, it is vital to retain some sense of time and place, for the importance of his contribution has waxed and waned with the years to a disconcerting degree.

Jazz has been evolving at an hysterical pace ever since people thought they heard Buddy Bolden say, and a displacement of a year or two in the evaluation of a piece of recorded work can reduce one's judgement to nonsense. Especially so is this true of Young, who has graduated from the blithe revolutionary of the 1930s with the Count Basie band, to the lethargic veteran of today. When faced with the daunting enormity of Young's retrospective reputation as a master, many commentators have, in judging his current work, either discounted him as a charlatan or merely paid lip-service to the legend. But in fact the task of evaluating him is little more than a matter of dates.

The latest Lester Young release, *Blue Lester* shows him in what musicians generally regard as his transition period, away from greatness into a gentle decline. This process, which began to be noticeable after Young and Basie parted company in the early 1940s, was finally complete by the end of the decade, by which time Young's significance as a figure on the jazz landscape had become that of a potent influence on the new generation of modern jazz musicians rather than that of an inspired executant.

Blue Lester contains several tracks recorded in 1944, and

23

a few which were made five years later. The listener, therefore, can play the intriguing game of trying to spot the modi-
fications in Young's style which took place during the five-
year lapse, and by so doing attempt to come to some closer
understanding of the nature of the achievement of one of the
most misunderstood jazz musicians in the history of the
music.

In some of the early tracks the remnants of the old master-
ful felicity occasionally flash through, as in Young's entry
into the tenor solo of 'Exercise in Swing'. This is the
authentic Lester Young of the quicksilver technique and
limitless powers of invention. But it is also the Lester Young
already embarked on his decline, for the tension of this solo
gradually slackens in a manner which would never have
happened a few years earlier.

The material Young uses on these tracks is a strong hint
to those who have still not solved the problem of whether
or not he is a modernist in the sense that the Charlie Parker-
Dizzy Gillespie generation were modernists. Young restricts
himself to elemental forms like the blues and 'I Got Rhythm',
or tunes like 'Indiana', which move in the conventional
pattern of resolving sevenths.

That Young could produce work like this at a time when
Charlie Parker was already casting aside the conventions of
improvisation which had been so meticulously observed in
Young's heyday, seems to prove once and for all that Young,
who after all did little to corrupt the harmonic innocence
of his times, was and is essentially a jazzman of the Swing
Age. One finds none of the chromatic progressions which are
the distinguishing feature of Parker's generation.

Despite this detachment of Young's *Blue Lester* gives
evidence of the fact that almost every tenor saxophonist of
today who means anything at all has plagiarised him un-
mercifully, although perhaps unconsciously, so integral a part
of the normal jazz vocabulary have Young's aphorisms become. He is the father-figure of modern tenor saxophone
playing, and no intelligent understanding of today's jazz is
possible without a close examination of his methods.

BEAULIEU 1958
The front lawn of the Palace House, Beaulieu, is not the
ideal spot for a jazz concert, not in the chill of a typical

English August night. The fingers of many musicians at Lord Montagu's two-day Jazz Festival were numb long before Friday's final chorus had been struck.

His Lordship did defy one British tradition, the one which says that jazz shows must always be either wholly traditional or wholly modern, and never a balance of the two. The Festival was begun by the fierce primitive enthusiasm of the Mick Mulligan band, supported by the eccentric baying of blues shouter George Melly, only to be continued by the equally fierce brilliance of the Jazz Couriers, the most vital of British modern groups. By the time the Couriers, led by two outstanding saxophonists, Ronnie Scott and Tubby Hayes, had finished their programme, several hundred connoisseurs had gathered on the lawn before the ingenious replica of a jazz-club bandstand, an affair in scaffolding and green canvas which somehow incorporated an authentic aura of tense light and fogged air, and was the most inspired piece of improvisation of the night.

From the start the crowd, young and mostly local, maintained a passivity auguring well for the future social standing of jazz fans. Nobody took advantage of conditions perfect for the perpetration of a little playful vandalism, and the two heavy truncheons on show in the entrance hall of the Palace House, 'used during the reign of William IV by the Special Constabulary', remained merely exhibits.

Most of the bill comprised the same familiar permutations of bands one sees every week-end in London, but there was one inspired selection. Featured with the Dill Jones Trio was trumpeter Nat Gonella, probably the first authentic British jazz musician ever. Considering that he played and sang Louis Armstrong standards like 'Shine' and 'I Can't Give You Anything But Love', and had been singing and playing them before most of those watching were born, Gonella's performance was surprisingly good. The crowd, many of whom must have wondered who he was (the official programme cost 2s, and you could buy two hotdogs, cooked over an open fire, for the same price), now began to wander about the grounds, partly to gratify curiosity, partly to restore blood circulation.

After the cheery informality of Jones and Gonella, the rehearsed and polished show of the Tommy Whittle Quintet was even more impressive than usual. In Whittle and Harry Klein patrons were seeing two saxophonists quite different in concept from Scott and Hayes, but just as effective in their own way. The pianist of this group, Eddie Thompson, played a solo of 'Love for Sale' which was the outstanding solo performance of the night.

Then came that curious gallimaufry, the Jazz Today Unit, a seven-piece group which perversely insisted on playing the jazz of yesterday, quite effectively, though its members found that as the evening temperature dropped, so did the pitch of their instruments. It took the unquenchable fires of the Mulligan band to brave the last twenty minutes before midnight, by which time many people had wandered off, still passive, no doubt intimidated by the profile of the Palace House, now firmly silhouetted by the moon.

They left behind them a lawn whose sundial, flower-beds and rustic seats were now augmented by bottles, glasses and what appeared to be the blunt ends of several hundred hot-dogs. By midnight, the festival organisers were breathing sighs of gratitude that the rain had held off, and speaking hopefully of a five thousand gate for the second big night of the festival, when the Johnny Dankworth Orchestra was booked for the front lawn.

BIRMINGHAM 1959
THE MODERNS ARE STILL STRUMMING
The student body has proved in the past to be far less progressive about its music than it is about most other things, but at this year's Inter-University Jazz Contest no fewer than twelve universities entered fourteen groups in the modern section of the competition. On hearing the entrants, it was not difficult to find reasons for this sudden upsurge in aspiration if not accomplishment.

Most of the groups who competed at Birmingham last week showed heavy influences of one of two groups from America which have toured Britain in the recent past, the Modern Jazz Quartet and the Dave Brubeck Quartet, and it seems clear that tours by American bands, banned by our Musicians' Union till three years ago, have captured the imagination of many students who might otherwise have continued to seek guidance merely from the record catalogues.

Most of the competing groups followed a pattern. Eight were quartets, which meant that little orchestration was called for. Most groups aped the more obvious mannerisms of either the Modern Jazz Quartet or Brubeck. The quartet from University College, Bangor, went one better and aped them both, one in each tune, and prefaced its performance of 'How High the Moon' (retitled 'Experiments with a Lunar Body') with a short explanatory lecture on cross-rhythms from its string bassist. Despite the lecture Bangor managed to come second.

I suspect that many of the musicians competing were converts from earlier styles of jazz, which would explain the depressing number of guitarists in the building. Every band included at least one guitarist and the Bristol University Quintet included two, billed on the programme as 'first' and 'second'. In British modern jazz the guitar has all but vanished as a solo instrument, for reasons which the contest at Birmingham made only too plain. The extreme technical mobility demanded by the modern style is beyond all but the very brilliant, and at Birmingham guitarist after guitarist lapsed into the good-natured strumming that was associated in my childhood with George Formby.

There were three attempts to make the kind of positive flourish that would win the contest, and the most eccentric of these came from the Oxford University Sextet, which reversed most of the conventional procedures. The leader is usually the only member privileged to stand up, but in the Oxford band he is the only member privileged to sit down. The two pieces the band played had wildly nonconformist titles, the first of which, 'My Dustbin is Full', was far more skilfully orchestrated than its name suggests. It was also evident from its performance that none of the present members of the Oxford band have ever heard of Zuleika Dobson, for although they were the only entrants who used feminine assistance, they used it in a most unchivalrous way. A very beautiful blonde, a vital cog in the Oxford jazz wheel, stood behind the piano throughout the performance holding up sheets of manuscript to guide the pianist, and hiding her own face in the process. She evoked more sympathy from the judges and more enthusiasm from the audience than any of the musicians who appeared.

A more desperate attempt at the imaginative gesture came from London University, who entered a fifteen-piece band playing the Basie theme, 'Swinging the Blues'. There is an old adage which says that the more players the easier it is to be out of tune, and the London University band, despite the presence of a lead alto saxophonist who displayed near-professional efficiency in his interpretation, found itself too encumbered ever to start.

The final attempt to impress came from the ten-piece entry from Cambridge University. In deference to their victory last year Cambridge were allowed to perform last, and the contemptuous ease with which they brushed aside all thirteen challengers suddenly made the contest appear hopelessly one-sided. For reasons which nobody has been able to explain to me, Cambridge has always had a long jazz lead over the other universities, and the virtuosity of this year's group may be conveyed by the fact that earlier in the evening it won the Traditional-Mainstream section of the competition. Its Modern performance showed real finesse and musical sensitivity. Only in showmanship was it bettered, and there Oxford and the blonde won hands down.

LONDON 1958
AMERICAN VISITORS

The visiting American season is upon us. Last week seven musicians arrived calling themselves the 'Jazz from Carnegie Hall' Group, a stratagem which fooled nobody. The 'Jazz from Carnegie Hall' Group is neither a group nor comes from Carnegie Hall, its component parts having been rustled up with little apparent consideration for group empathy.

The 'Carnegie Hall' tour, which still has half its course to run, typifies those which overwhelm audiences by sheer starpower. Each of its seven members has won his place in the harrowing world of popularity polls and long-playing releases, and six of them are emerging triumphant from this tour. This is an abnormally high average, for concert tours usually prove disastrous for established reputations made on record; jazz musicians are for some mysterious reason best heard and not seen.

The sole failure of this tour so far has been the alto saxophonist, Lee Konitz, the one musician thought likely to prove indifferent to alien environments, eccentric acoustics and an unfamiliar rhythm section. But the experience seems to have been too much for him, and several times last week during the four London concerts he was reduced by his own painful sensibilities to complete silence, nervously adjusting his mouthpiece and casting hasty glances over his shoulder at a sturdy rhythm section which could do no more to help him out of his dilemma.

Konitz, once the *enfant terrible* of modern jazz saxophonists, seems now to have passed into dotage without any intervening period of maturity. All week he has stood woebegone, and faltering, separated from his fellows by a barrier of introspection which has horrified his idolaters and perhaps compensated those who never quite forgave him ten years ago for refusing to copy Charlie Parker.

The other saxophonist, Zoot Sims, whose inflated embouchure would have tempted Adolphe Sax to throw up his hands in distraction, is the diametric opposite of Konitz, unconcernedly extrovert, and what was known in F. Scott Fitzgerald days as a 'playing fool'. His work is uncommonly free from all frippery. Every note has some structural significance, which gives his solos a strength and boldness rare in jazz. He possesses none of the feline subtlety of his old comrade Stan Getz, who came here last season, but the candour of his expression and his forthright method have proved a profound relief after the irresolution of Konitz.

The biggest popular success of the tour has been the trombone duets of Jay Jay Johnson and Kai Winding, two men of astonishing technical expertise and melodic ingenuity. Their duets are presented in the simplest possible form. A short introduction, a statement of the theme, sometimes in unison, sometimes harmonised quite simply, and then a succession of solos. The sparseness of the approach makes heavy demands on the imagination, but both Johnson and Winding have succeeded with no apparent effort in sustaining interest throughout the second half of the programme.

Even their quoting has not been the usual quoting. The average jazz concert audience is peculiarly prone to the Quote. A single phrase from 'Whistle While You Work' or 'Umbrella Man', and it instantly feels impelled to applaud and reduce itself to drooling sycophancy.

Johnson and Winding, however, threw in their quotes at such a whirlwind pace, and amid such a welter of melodic invention, that too often the audience missed the allusions altogether. Johnson began by slipping in the clarinet figure from 'Peter and the Wolf', which inspired Winding to reply with a snatch from 'Carmen', followed by some cunningly worked-in Stephen Foster. Johnson then fell back on his own environment with echoes of 'Dardanella' and 'Hawaiian War Chant'.

So far the tour has been a moderate success, although perhaps the mildness of critical reaction is connected in some way with the fact that next month the fun really begins with the belated arrival here with entourage and full orchestra, after twenty-five years, of Duke Ellington.

GEORGE LEWIS, 1959
JAZZ ECHOES OF THE PAST

The British tour of George Lewis's New Orleans Band, lasting throughout January, is one of those events which underline the breathless haste of jazz evolution. While the rest of the arts have been cooking over a slow fire for a few thousand years, jazz has been thrust into the pressure cooker of contemporary life, so that it has moved from primitivism to neo-classicism in fifty years.

To the modernist George Lewis's clarinet-playing presents the same problems that a buffalo might to Sitting Bull's grandson. Lewis is an authentic New Orleans antique whose experience stretches back into the semi-mythology of street parades, band contests and the Storyville red light district. And yet there he was last Sunday, almost as large as life on the stage of the Odeon Theatre, Tottenham Court Road, taking over where the Wyatt Earp entourage had left off the day before.

The ages of the six members of the Lewis band are sometimes disputed, but it is generally accepted that the string bassist Alcide 'Slow Drag' Pavageau was born in 1888. Lewis himself is a callow youth of fifty-nine, while the extreme youth of trumpeter Avery Howard, born in 1908, is underlined by his professional name 'Kid'.

Lewis plays in an uncorrupted turn-of-the-century manner, recalling the days when jazz was the do-it-yourself music of an oppressed minority dumped in an alien society. It is here, on the fringes of the sociologist's world, that the value of Lewis's performance really lies. By strict musical standards his band is abysmal. Intonation is hopelessly at sea. Technical limitations cripple the soloists, and the lead given by 'Kid' Howard is so weak as to be at times literally inaudible. Melodic conceptions are rudimentary and the triad of the tonic major appears again and again in the improvisations of Lewis himself, the most articulate of the six.

The appeal lies elsewhere, in the miraculously preserved artistic naïveté of musicians who were active before their music had begun to travel up-river to St Louis and Chicago, artists whose repertoire of over 500 themes creates echoes of a vanished past in classics like 'Dallas Blues', 'Canal Street Blues', 'Georgia Camp Meeting' and 'Corrine Corrine'.

The mystique which envelops this kind of revivalism in jazz has created for its audiences hungrier for the legends than for the music which inspired them, audiences unaware either of the serious limitations of the Lewis method or of the place this kind of jazz style has in the history of the music. The sentimental cultist following of Lewis in this country is tremendous, and the explanation lies in the very shortcomings of the music. The jazz past is receding swiftly. Soon there will be none of the New Orleans originals left, hence the craving to examine the unspoilt article while it still exists.

The power of the cult was most effectively demonstrated by the supporting band of British musicians, Ken Colyer and his Band, bearded men in their twenties who have aped the mannerisms of men like Lewis with an unhealthy fanaticism. Indeed, part of Colyer's appeal lies in the fact that as a merchant seaman he was once incarcerated in a New Orleans prison.

The comment I heard on Lewis's performance while leaving the theatre, that it was an assault on the ears, may have had some relevance, but I feel it was unfair. One does not expect a milestone to start walking along the road. Lewis's band is simply a perfect embalming job, and one must learn to approach it with that fact very much in mind. Apart from all else, it is a form of musical expression which will make the fingers of every self-respecting musicologist twitch with fascination.

VICTOR FELDMAN 1960
RETURN OF THE PRODIGAL
Britain being no more than a very far-flung outpost of the jazz empire, a dilemma confronts the local boy who makes good in the international sense. Once or twice Europeans have achieved standards of form and content which compare favourably with those of their American contemporaries, and each time the choice facing them has been to go west or wither.

The reason is that jazz music, an act of individual expression, is paradoxically the one art in which the musician is chained by the sheer mechanics of music making, to the limitations of those who comprise the groups he plays with. For a gifted European, there must come a time when he senses that no longer can be find adequate support or inspiration from those around him. In Britain the musician usually turns his back on the problem, content perhaps to be a big fish in a rather small pool. This month British listeners have the chance to judge for themselves whether a migration pays the aesthetic dividends to justify such a drastic measure.

Victor Feldman, a musician of truly extraordinary potential, left for San Francisco five years ago, and is currently appearing at Ronnie Scott's Club, Gerrard Street, W. At the time he left Britain, Feldman was recognised by fellow-musicians who had worked with him over long periods, as a jazz player of the highest class. His history as a professional almost smacked of Hollywood.

Feldman was discovered by his own brothers to be a natural drummer at the age of seven, the only real prodigy jazz has ever produced. At fifteen he switched to the piano, and, to the delight of the British jazz world, added the gifts of melody and harmony to talents which had so far been assumed to be purely rhythmic. Before he left he had also developed into a promising composer of original themes. After five years, American musicians, and even their critics, recognise Feldman as one of the two or three vibraphonists in jazz of real stature. The question must now be faced by those of us at home who have the opportunity to hear him again, exactly how and to what extent Feldman's self-imposed exile has benefited him musically.

The advantages of his actions would seem to be psychological as much as musical, for apart from the natural processes of gathering maturity – Feldman is still only in his middle twenties – he has developed a self-assurance which adds to the poise of his performances and gives noticeable encouragement to those fortunate enough to be playing with him on this visit. Particularly impressive are the astonishing stop-choruses in which he often indulges. Midway through a solo, the entire rhythm section is cut out, and Feldman plays two or three choruses unaccompanied. It is a gambit currently very popular among modern musicians desperately seeking variations on all too familiar themes. Feldman performs this difficult feat with wonderful musical awareness, for besides sustaining melodic interest he implies both the harmonic and rhythmic underpinning of what he is playing with great subtlety. One possible indication of his future development is perhaps found in his piano-playing, where he indulges far less in single lines in the right hand, playing instead long successions of richly harmonised passages.

He is the most gifted jazz musician Britain has ever produced, and his current London appearances suggest that today he must be included among the finest instrumentalists in the world.

LOUIS 1960
TRUMPETERS THREE

Somebody once pointed out that the Louis Armstrong Hot Five recordings which changed the course of jazz, occupied seventeen days in the working life of a professional musician, and that the permanence of wax had misled everybody into exaggerating their importance to Armstrong himself, to whom they were merely an incident in a vast career. On the other hand there is no reason to suppose that the recordings caught Armstrong in a peculiarly exalted mood. No doubt he performed miracles every day, and *Louis Armstrong – The Greatest Years, Volume One,* sounds like substantial proof.

Armstrong made these sixteen recordings in 1926, and once they were committed to wax, jazz thought was never the same. With performances like 'King of the Zulus', 'Who'sit' and 'Muskrat Ramble', the virtuoso soloist began to come into his own, and the convention of collective improvisation was slowly abandoned. The development was inevitable, so soon as the jazz environment threw up a musician too prolific to be contained by the ensemble.

By 1926 Armstrong was a young giant bursting out of a cage too puny to hold him. The process was gradual, and in the period covered by the first of the four planned Armstrong revivals, he was still observing the letter if not the spirit of the ensemble conception. But time reveals the truth of his vast superiority to his four fellow-musicians, and the inevitability of the day when he would cease to be limited by them.

The remarkable thing about the trumpet-playing on this album is the apparent simplicity of its greatness. Armstrong is drawing on only a few harmonies, and he respects the conventions of discord and resolution religiously. And yet the music he produces sounds benign, heroic, even profound. It took a revolution in harmonic thought to produce anything as original or as beautiful, and that revolution was a long time coming. When it did come, its leaders showed an unfortunate propensity to get themselves killed off before they had begun.

The Fabulous Fats Navarro is a reminder of the grace of one of the earliest modern pioneers, a grace that was precocious because in the 1940s modernists had still not formulated their own conventions. Navarro, who died in 1950 in his twenty-seventh year, was less exhibitionistic than his contemporary Dizzy Gillespie, about whose playing there was something almost mechanistic. Navarro had a ravishing tone and a precise delivery which has tempted many hacks to the metaphor of bullets from a gun.

Considering the chaotic musical world he inhabited, he seems to have been extraordinarily sure of himself. His solos have a poise which belies the infancy of the music he was pioneering, almost as though they had been planned beforehand. And perhaps they were, for the alternate takes of 'The Squirrel' bear striking resemblance.

Navarro's trail-blazing bore fruit soon after his death when Clifford Brown began recording. Brown's technique was reminiscent of Navarro's, with its strings of even quavers spat out with intensity and precision, but he was harmonically far more subtle. The *Clifford Brown Memorial* includes ten examples of Brown's incomparable gift for resolving the complexities of modern harmony into melodic coherence, drawing for his phrases on everything from his own inventive powers to an old Ellington theme called 'A Blues Serenade'.

Brown was killed in a car smash in 1956 when he was twenty-six. His recordings suggest that with his death modern jazz lost one of the very few soloists whose buoyancy was not punctured by the esoteric harmonic tricks of the day. In 'Brownie Speaks', there is no trace of a frown in the trumpet-playing. On the contrary Brown actually makes the instrument laugh and sing at the sheer joy of making jazz, just as Armstrong was doing thirty years before.

CHRISTIAN 1961
In modern circles there is usually a reverential hush when anybody mentions Minton's the uptown New York club

where, twenty years ago a small nucleus of musicians began the casual experiments which slowly emerged into the phenomenon of bebop. The men who contributed at Minton's were by no means the cohesive group that the legends says they were. The bulk of the music played there was more conventional than we have been led to believe, and the belated issue in this country of *The Harlem Jazz Scene, 1941*, is likely to cloud the issue still further.

The Harlem album features Charlie Christian on one side and Dizzie Gillespie on the other, and is comprised exclusively of the kind of jazz we associate with the inchoate days of modernism. But Minton's was also the stamping ground of the great Swing Age stylists like Ben Webster, Roy Eldridge and Lester Young, which explains why none of the music in 'The Harlem Jazz Scene' contains all the elements of modernism. The soloist had to take whatever rhythm section he could get, so that time and again one is struck by the incongruity between Gillespie's revolutionary thought and the naïve plodding of those around him.

Christian was an even more curious case. His professional career was ended almost before it began. A year or so with the Benny Goodman Orchestra and then a depressingly early death. Incarcerated as he was in the very stronghold of the conventional jazz of the day, Christian contrived to use his spare time playing the kind of music which in a few years had completely replaced the cadences of the Goodman era. It is not surprising that there is a certain dichotomy in his thought in 'The Harlem Jazz Scene'. Although his melodic invention is spiced with dramatic originality, much of the content is simply the familiar phraseology of the day. It remains one of the riddles of jazz whether Christian, had he lived a little longer, would have resolved the conflict.

His guitar playing heard across the years, remains amazing, brilliant, effortless, charged with a more subtle kind of electricity than the power which amplified the strings of his instrument. Had he been able to use suitable material then he might have sounded even more apocalyptic than he did. But those were early days, and the material simply did not exist.

Six years later there was a wealth of it, and in *Diz 'n Bird in Concert*, Gillespie and Charlie Parker revel in it. By now Gillespie has clearly resolved his problems of style. In the 1941 recordings there are still strong traces of the influence of Roy Eldridge, but six years later Gillespie has already founded a new style, and has also discovered how to write themes to suit that style. 'Groovin' High' is typical of his subterfuge. Taking a hoary favourite like 'Whispering', Gillespie threw the melody aside and borrowed the harmonies to construct a fresh melody recognisable only to the most literate of musicians as a close relative of a Jazz Age song like 'Whispering'.

Even Gillespie, with all his dazzle, is eclipsed by the saxophonist Charlie Parker, just as complex harmonically as Dizzy, but far less mechanistic in his melodic construction. Somehow Parker managed to incorporate within the frame of his style all the new devices and still manage to restore to jazz the simplicity of emotional expression it had lost during the 1930s. That is why the second half of the album, featuring a Gillespie Sextet without Parker, circa 1953, is an anti-climax.

It represents the third and last stage in the birth of modern jazz. With Christian, the idiom is struggling to be born. In the Parker concert sides the style is approaching maturity. In the Gillespie Sextet tracks, the artist is looking for an audience. There is questionable comedy, silly flippant vocals, and the bitter acknowledgement that in an indifferent world, jazz itself is not enough, even when it is Christian's or Parker's jazz. The familiar cycle has begun once more, back to the comic hats and the false noses.

GOODMAN 1962

As the evolving complexities of contemporary jazz make ever-increasing demands on the ingenuity of the soloist, so the Swing Age, that period of melodic giants and comparative harmonic innocence, begins to acquire a nostalgic appeal which sometimes seems about to degenerate into a sentimental morass. Jazz fanciers dream of obscure, untabulated recordings being unearthed and belatedly issued, hoping that there may be found fresh epigrams from Lester Young, further flights of brilliant fancy from Benny Goodman, unheard apocalyptic visions from Charlie Christian. And now the dream materialises in the form of a double issue called *Spirituals to Swing*.

The 'Spirituals to Swing' concerts were held in Carnegie

Hall, the first in December, 1938, the second and last a year later, and the musicians who participated represent the most adventurous spirits of the times. It is important to make this point, because devotees of post-war jazz tend to forget that modernism is not a style but an attitude, and that Young, Goodman, Christian and the rest were the progressives of their day.

The programmes were arranged by John Hammond, a unique figure in jazz, an inspired amateur whose judgement was so good that he was personally responsible for the presentation to wider audiences of then unknown or little-known coloured artistes like Christian, Billie Holiday, and Count Basie.

At the time of the Carnegie Hall concerts Young and Christian were both at the height of their powers, and the tracks on which they play together are among the finest and most rare of all jazz recordings. 'Good Morning Blues', and 'Way Down Yonder in New Orleans' give the listener the opportunity to hear that it was Lester Young who epitomised the harmonic conventions of the day and Charlie Christian who was the first of the pre-war soloists with some inkling of the modernism to come. In contrast the maestro, Benny Goodman, sounds quite venerable, although the tracks featuring his sextet are woefully under-recorded.

The two albums are crammed with revelatory matter. There is a rare Count Basie piano solo of 'Ain't Got Nobody', which might surprise those who know Basie only for his understatements with his big orchestra. There are two towering performances from the father of stride piano, James P. Johnson, some vintage soprano saxophone playing from Sidney Bechet, a tantalising glimpse of the full Basie band in the days of its greatness, and some priceless singing from the Golden Gate Quartet and Mitchell's Christian Singers.

For once the albums are annotated with real intelligence and sensitivity, complete with eye-witness accounts of the concerts. It would be madness to nominate a single track from this wealth of material, but the free-for-all which takes place on 'Lady be Good' offers more relevant information as to the respective merits of the best jazzmen of the period than a dozen treatises.

The albums are a monument to Hammond's perseverance and devotion to the cause. Before he succeeded he was to suffer many setbacks. He tells in his notes, 'Robert Johnson, blues singer and guitarist, was signed, and then was promptly murdered in a Mississippi bar-room brawl, whereupon Big Bill Broonzy was prevailed upon to leave his Arkansas farm and mule and make his very first trek to the Big City.'

Bubbles

The section which follows deals with one of the most extraordinary episodes in jazz history, and one which perhaps marks a watershed, not only of the music, but of public attitudes towards it. One of jazz's great compensations for being a music too esoteric for marketing on a mass scale was that it had usually been left unattended by the makers of fashion, who had found their sensibilities, if that is the word, more easily attuned to hit parades, dance bands and night club cabaret. But by the sheer law of averages, it was perhaps inevitable that one day the trendsetters should batten on to jazz as a new diversion, distort its values, upset its criteria, smother it with wet kisses before leaving it to die of confusion. The makers of fashion took a long time to make their move, and it was laughably predictable that when they did, the objects of their affection should be a pair of extremely astute piano-playing publicists whose musical effects ranged from excessive politeness to the playful roar of a paper tiger.

Twenty years after the event it is difficult to convey the intensity of the furore of devotion for the Modern Jazz Quartet and the Dave Brubeck Quartet displayed by tremulous acolytes who had, until that very moment, mysteriously managed to control their passion for jazz to the extent of not bothering with it at all. Tens of thousands of people who all their lives had believed Bix to be some kind of breakfast food and Ellington the victor of Waterloo suddenly discovered that overnight the grace of art had been bestowed upon them.

I do not question the sincerity of their devotionals, even though at the time many of them questioned the sincerity of mine. Such miraculous conversions as took place at the jazz concerts of the period have been known to occur periodically throughout recorded history, usually in an atmosphere whose religious ecstasy has discouraged the exercise of dispassionate

39

thought, and it was precisely such an atmosphere, compounded in equal parts of piety and adoration, which prevailed the moment either Brubeck or John Lewis, the leader of the Modern Jazz Quartet, so much as poked his nose round a safety curtain. What I was questioning then, and still question now, is whether anyone can hope to arrive at valid conclusions about an artistic performance without having first acquired its historical frame of reference. How could a man be confident that what Brubeck and Lewis were playing broke new ground when he had never been taken over the old? What could they know of Brubeck, these new zealots, who only Brubeck knew? It really was extremely clever of them.

My predicament at the time was complicated by the fact that never once did I attend any of the performances reviewed below without ensuring the companionship of a few friends better informed as to the jazz art than I was. I suppose after all these years it does no harm to confess that I attended the Brubeck and Lewis recitals insulated from errors of judgement in this way, and that many of the opinions I later expressed in print were not mine, or at least had come to be mine at second hand. Probably it was professionally unethical of me, but frankly I had no choice. Each time I sat down to attend to the religious ceremonies conducted by Brubeck and Lewis I was surrounded by a whole battalion of emissaries who had been my boon companions for so long that I would have known of no way to detach myself from them even had I wanted to, which I most certainly did not. In retrospect I suppose it was grossly unfair of me to have taken with me to these concerts the shades of Bix and Louis, Hawkins and Lester, Bechet and Tatum, but there was nothing unusual in this. Every working musician I knew was in the identical predicament, of not being able to help relating what he was hearing with what he had once heard. And what I was now hearing seemed so trivial that the moment the music began and the zealots to genuflect, the invisible host at my side began first to laugh, then to scratch itself, and finally to drift off in search of the nearest bar.

Brubeck was a new phenomenon in jazz, a perennial student who had never worked in anybody's group but his own. This in itself was no disqualification, although it was silly to pretend it was much help. It seemed to me that he played the piano so clumsily, and with such consistent clumsiness, that from the day I first attended one of his performances, my impatience was tempered by a touch of that compassion which one usually feels at the spectacle of a fellow-musician flung by circumstances into a hopelessly false position. For either Brubeck chose to accept the myth of his own infallibility, or he did not, each of the options being worse than the other, either to accept the reality of a genius he did not in fact possess, or be obliged to strive hopelessly for it every time he confronted a keyboard. At first I was surprised that such footling juvenilia should be taken even halfway seriously by those who knew of Art Tatum and Bud Powell. Slowly my surprise was replaced by wry acceptance of the fact that possibly those who knew of Tatum and Powell and still took Brubeck seriously did not know of Tatum and Powell after all. When Big Ben strikes thirteen, it has been pointed out, we are informed by the conviction, not only that Big Ben is hopelessly wrong now, but that it must also have been hopelessly wrong in all the years we accepted its findings in good faith.

Attendance at Brubeck concerts for me became a nightmare which I would not have missed for worlds. The images were too rich to pass over, of Brubeck falling deeper and deeper into the rut of some wretched cross-rhythm, digging a pit for himself with such relentless determination that soon he falls into it and disappears from view; Brubeck climbing out again and arriving at the same juncture of a song for six or seven successive choruses, 'improvising' the same phrase each time; Brubeck shyly telling us that what he is now about to play is more or less impossible, but that he is going to be very gallant and play it anyway.

We met only once, long after the Brubeck era was over, when he emerged from semi-retirement to appear in a BBC television series for which I had been hired as the compère. An hour before filming was due to begin, I was led down the dining-room of the auditorium and introduced to him at his table, where, until my arrival, he had been enjoying a light meal. He seemed a mild-mannered man, and as he caught my name he visibly, if only momentarily, flinched. As he did so, the recollection sprang to mind of what a mutual friend had once told me, that Brubeck, having suffered a few of my reviews in silence, had arrived finally at the conclusion that my detestation for his playing must have some obscure personal motivation, which seemed to me to imply an artistic vanity of truly comic proportions. To put it another way, he

simply could not accept the posibility that anyone could dis-
like his music so violently as I appeared to do. I sat down
facing him, remarking 'I come in peace', and spent the next
ten minutes in pleasant discussion of how I might reconcile
my critical instinct to batter him with my temporary obligation to flatter him, although as my announcement at the opening of his recital was limited to one minute, the problem
virtually solved itself. A few days later the auditorium burnt
to the ground, but I have no reason to believe that this
tragedy was connected in any way with our meeting. Today,
without the physical presence of his studious personality to
buttress it, Brubeck's legend is already disappearing into the
middle distance. Posterity may well wonder how such a
legend should have come about in the first place.

John Lewis and the Modern Jazz Quartet were an altogether different propositon. I have always felt that Brubeck
played the way he did because he could not help himself.
The heart of the matter was simply not in him. Appearances
suggest that it was not in John Lewis either, but for once,
and for an extremely interesting reason, it may just be that
appearances are deceptive. Normally in jazz they never are.
What a man plays is the sole accurate barometer, and what
he believes, or says he believes, remains an irrelevance.
He may belittle other musicians, as Benny Goodman and
Louis Armstrong once belittled the new modernists; he may
question the purity of their artistic souls, as Gary Burton
once did Stan Getz's; he may draw ridiculous analogies between their playing and Gabriel's, as Muggsy Spanier once
did in reference to Tommy Ladnier. None of it matters.
Nothing a musician says, no attitude he strikes, no philosophy
to which he subscribes, can invalidate the truth to nature of
what he plays. But John Lewis may just possibly be the one
exception, the sole example in jazz history of a man who
thought himself and talked himself and attitudinised himself
out of mastery. I do not believe it myself, but I offer it as a
possibility if only in deference to Lewis's position. The case he
represents is a very odd one.

As far as I have been able to deduce, from his general behaviour as well as from his playing, Lewis believes jazz to be
vulgar. More than one mutual acquaintance over the years
has quoted remarks by Lewis to this effect, but I would not
be inclined to attach much weight to them were it not for
the striking consistency with which they substantiate the
evidence of the music. Lewis's dream has been to purge

jazz of all indecencies, all coarser overtones, all unfortunate rabelaisian gestures, which is certainly a thoroughly praise-worthy ambition, always provided that in cleansing her soul you do not make the same mistake as Othello and fracture her windpipe at the same time. There can be no argument that in a strictly limited sense, Lewis's bowdlerising campaign has flourished famously. No music by the Modern Jazz Quartet has even been tainted by even the faintest hint of vulgarity. Its mannerisms of dress and its stage deportment may have been garish, but of vulgarity in the music itself there has never been so much as a faint suspicion. Indeed, that is the trouble with it. For in his attempts to distil the decorous essence, Lewis has refined jazz out of existence, which raises the question, vulgar in comparison to what? And once we find the answer it seems plain that Lewis is yet another victim of a common American cultural complaint, familiar enough in the arts generally but unprecedented in jazz. From somewhere, perhaps in his studies in anthropology at the University of New Mexico, Lewis has caught a chronic case of Jamesian obsession with Europe.

From its beginning the MJQ paraded titles whose foreign overtones were presumably intended to make them appear more significant. The first two sides by the group I ever heard, purchased from the meagre funds of a co-operative jazz band of which I was a serving member, were titled 'The Queen's Fancy' and 'Delauney's Dilemma'. The dynasty of the queen was unspecified, but it was clear that her postures were vaguely English, vaguely medieval and vaguely Tennysonian, and therefore, presumably, vaguely spurious. Delauney was a French jazz critic. I found the sides very pleasant, but representative of nothing more than a charming little backwater, certainly not of the brave new world of syncopation. But things got much worse after that. At least those first two titles had been in English. It was not always to be so; Milano, Versailles, Fontessa, La Ronde, Vendome, Baden-Baden, Cortege, La Cantatrice. Sometimes the music created a mood which approximated to the implications of its title. Sometimes it did not. The interesting thing was that by annexing a few venerable titles, Lewis won for his music the same polite respect that the titles themselves had earned over the centuries, although why he should find the decrepi-tude of Venice more congenial than the decrepitude of New Orleans remains a mystery. The MJQ has been playing this game for nearly twenty years now and has evidently still not tired of it. While revising this volume for the printers, I attended a performance by the group in which there was included a piece which was supposed to have parallels with the *Commedia dell'arte*, because both contained an element of improvisation. So does a football match, but Lewis is unlikely to give us a composition describing one.

Lewis's tactics earned the MJQ a prestige so prodigious that in its heyday many people considered even mild criticism to be verging on the sacrilegious. Nor was all of this adulation due to mere cultural snobbery. A great deal of it was, but not all of it. For not only were the titles of the MJQ's repertoire attractive in the way they struck exactly the right balance between the familiar and the inscrutable, but the music itself was reassuring in a way that much of the best work of a Charlie Parker or a Duke Ellington was not. Musicians like Parker and Ellington might well tempt you into deep waters and then leave you to drown, but the worst that could happen to you at the hands of the MJQ was that your feet might get a bit wet. Like all abstract art forms, jazz can present a forbidding face to the uninitiated. It offers no convenient toeholds, no extra-musical points of reference. But here was a group which often gave you a broad hint as to what the music was supposed to be describing. In which case, why had Ellington who, with his suites and his thumbnail sktches, had been doing precisely this for years, and doing it infinitely better, never been accorded the same reverence from audiences? I don't know why.

It used to be said in defence of the MJQ that even if its jazz bona fides were suspect, at least it was drawing into the jazz fold thousands of don't-knows who might otherwise have been lost to the cause, and who might, now that Lewis had initiated them, graduate to better things. This may well have been so, but there was just as much to be said for the opposite case, which is that for those weaned on the liquorice water of the MJQ, a sip of anything stronger might easily kill them stone dead. And as I sat there each time, with my invisible friends at my side, the group's pretensions never failed to appear idiotic.

Perhaps the most predictable price to be paid for this reaction of mine was the breaking off of diplomatic relations. Once my sentiments on the group appeared in print, Lewis wanted no part of me, professionally or otherwise. The night before my first review appeared, we met for the first and, as it proved, the last time, at one of those Saturday night parties where the identity of the host and the purpose of the event are mysteries so inscrutable that nobody bothers to try solving them. Lewis, quietly euphoric after his rapturous reception earlier that evening, stood chatting over a table of salad, cheeses and loaves of bread. (Knowing his predilection for things European, I was happy for him that they were loaves of French bread.) We were introduced by Chris Barber, and I was still naïve enough in those days not to feel any fraudulence in the heartiness of my handshake. The knowledge that in an hour or two my review would be on sale did not inhibit my enjoyment of the food or the small talk. Why should it inhibit his? I remember doubting to myself whether he even bothered to read reviews, or if he did, to take them with any degree of seriousness. But he did.

On his next visit he was invited to appear on a television arts programme, in which he would be asked some pertinent questions. But not, apparently, too pertinent, because after I had been invited to appear as his inquisitor, the word came back that he insisted on someone else, at which I withdrew with commendable good grace and somebody else was found to knock up a few polite conversational services across the sagging net of Lewis's vanity. That was several years ago, and we have never been in any kind of contact since nor, I suppose, ever will.

Nor do I have much doubt that when we are both pushing up daisies, our respective executors will see to it that we are separated in the execution of that harmless horticultural function by numberless green fields. A sad loss, but perhaps for the best. In any case, I am well used to such situations. Benny Goodman once cheered me up immeasurably by letting it be known he wanted nothing to do with me, and Gary Burton once wrote a letter expressing the impatience with which he anticipated attending my last rites. So be it. On the other hand Stan Getz and I once had an extremely enjoyable and altogether amicable discussion about an unfavourable review of his playing I had recently composed. And once, Duke Ellington, in referring to an essay I had written about him, fed me the back-handed compliment, 'My friends tell me it was well-written', as if to let me know he had no intention of ever reading it for himself. And quite right too. If I could make music half as well as Ellington can, I wouldn't waste my time reading reviews either.

BRUBECK 1959
RHODE ISLAND RONDOS
The British jazz-fan is highly conscious of his own insularity.
He yearns to be in the swim, so our promoters cater most
thoughtfully for this desire by sticking topical labels on their
American touring shows. The current party of barnstormers
are masquerading under the banner of 'Jazz From Newport',
the Newport in question being a place in Rhode Island which
is the venue of the world's most heavily attended jazz festival.

It is true that the three American groups which comprise
this package show have all appeared at the Newport Festival,
but then so has everybody else. From the sound of the music
at the opening concert at the Royal Festival Hall last week-
end, perhaps the word vaudeville might have been included
somewhere in the billing.

The three attractions represent a fascinating historical
cross-section of jazz, with the Buck Clayton band belonging
to pre-war Swing days, and the Dizzy Gillespie Quintet to
the early times of the modernist revolution, while the Dave
Brubeck Quartet may be described as one of the peculiar
aberrations of current taste. The promoters, perhaps with a
sly sense of humour, arranged the programme backwards, with
Brubeck hammering the audience into submission, Gillespie
milking it indiscriminately for laughs, and Clayton sending
it home half-believing that jazz really is what it used to be,
which, of course, it certainly is not.

Dave Brubeck is a pianist with supreme faith in his
own method, which is to blind us all with the science of elementary musical terminology. One of his pieces, he proudly
told us, is a Turkish folk tune with the traditional blues form
superimposed upon it, the whole being in the traditional
European rondo form. As nobody present knew any Turkish
folk tunes, or had any idea what the traditional European
rondo form consisted of, all were warmed by Brubeck's subtle
flattery. It is an alarming thought, but the Brubeck Quartet,
ostensibly a jazz group, played a programme which completely abandoned the four-beats-to-a-bar pulse which everybody used to think was an essential ingredient of jazz.

Brubeck, in introducing works written in three-four and
five-four time, is no doubt attempting to free the music from
what Chesterton once described as 'that undercurrent of

battering monotony which I believe is supposed to be one of the charms of jazz.' Escape from the prison of the rhythmic pattern of jazz is all very well but the Brubeck Quartet has bestowed upon itself so much freedom that it has become hopelessly lost in it.

The Dizzy Gillespie group which followed Brubeck was expected to restore something like order to the proceedings, but Gillespie, a highly gifted musician and a virtuoso trumpeter, also happens to be an indifferent comic, and from the moment he made his entrance sporting some obscure kind of eastern headwear, it was evident it was laughs he was after. His act, for an act it certainly was, comprised an incongruous mixture of wonderful jazz and uninspired buffoonery. A trumpet chorus of extreme technical brilliance and moving sensitivity might be followed by leg-cocking and eyebrowwagging which scored nervous laughter and ruined the musical mood.

When the Buck Clayton band took over, expectations rose hopefully once more, and were at least partly fulfilled. The Clayton band is formed of veterans from the pre-war Count Basie band and on several of these men the years sit lightly indeed. Clayton played trumpet solos which sounded naïve after Gillespie, but because of their very *naïveté,* highly relaxing. The five-strong ensemble sound was unpolished but exciting and the final appearance of blues singer Jimmie Rushing brought the concert to a real, as distinct from an academic, climax. When Mr Rushing appeared, Mr Brubeck's claims for the rondo form finally manifested themselves, for Mr Rushing is a squat barrel of a man more perfectly rondo in form than anything that ever came out of the Royal Academy. He has a minimal vocal range, very cleverly improvises a broad melody into an almost flat line, and succeeds through his enormous enthusiasm and a faultless feeling for the blues idiom.

I would be most interested to know what Mr Rushing made of Mr Brubeck's explanatory announcements, or the pietistic compèring of an American gentleman called Willis Conover. Mr Conover, who looks like a Madison Avenue prototype, spoke with a dead pan of the conscious in jazz, the sub-conscious in jazz, the unconscious in jazz, its dancing feet, its white tie and tails, and a great deal else, which, as it sounded highly impressive and meant hardly anything, was word music not far behind that of Jimmie Rushing himself.

MJQ 1959
THOSE VICTORIAN BLUES

The Modern Jazz Quartet is one of the most astonishing cultural phenomena of the post-war period. For the last five years four men have sought with painful eagerness to transform the racy art of jazz into something aspiring towards cultural respectability. The photographs on the covers of their best-selling albums show three bearded men and one bespectacled man in morning-coats, looking at the camera with the studied gloom of four eminent Victorians who have just heard about 'The Origin of Species'.

The attempt of their pianist, John Lewis, to make jazz socially acceptable is an excellent idea. Better morning-coats and gloom than tales of Al Capone and bootleg days. The snag is that this courting of respectability has drained away so much of the vitality of their music that there is little left but a few flickers of animation from the brilliant vibraharpist, Milt Jackson, and occasional passages reminiscent of Bach of all people.

The group's instrumentation is piano, drums, bass and vibraharp. The sound is necessarily so introspective that ten minutes after the opening of their concert in the Festival Hall last Saturday one became acutely conscious that the quartet had only two degrees of dynamics, soft and very soft. The earthiness of jazz has been replaced by a fey tinkling which sounds inadequate when the quartet treat traditional forms like the Blues, and even worse in rendering original compositions like Lewis's three sketches of characters from the *Commedia dell'arte,* blended into a suite called 'Comedy'.

Lewis's integrity as a jazz musician is unquestioned. He has vast experience as a pianist with most of the outstanding soloists of the last ten years. He has decided, however, that jazz must become international in the sense that it must be made to portray people and places generally considered incompatible with jazz. Most of his theme titles are French, although there is rarely much connection between the title and the music. The one essential element in any jazz performance, the preservation of the illusion of improvisation, he has cast to the winds, pursuing instead rarer and rarer refinement, like a man attempting to gain entry into an enchanted garden.

There was one moment during the concert when the irony of the situation would have been enough to make a cat laugh. The group played a tune written by Duke Ellington called 'It Don't Mean a Thing if it Ain't Got that Swing'. The tune is one which respects the edict of its own title, being constructed in such a way that provided it is taken at the intended tempo, it cannot possibly be played in a dull manner. Or so I would have thought. The quartet did a better job of musical demolition on Ellington's theme than any other group, band or orchestra I have come across. They meddled with the time-values of the notes unpardonably, and in their interpretation of the harmonies proved yet again that for all their good intentions, and the courage and resource with which they put them into practice, the extreme limitations of their tone colouring renders them impotent much of the time.

The National Jazz Federation augumented the quartet with two British saxophonists whose comparative vulgarisms tore the unity of the quartet into shreds, although it was hardly their fault. The quartet plays music from the twilight corridors of a dream, and saxophones have no place there. The reaction of British audiences has been hysterical, audiences comprising the same people who abandoned Ellington to half-empty houses last year. My own feelings coincide with those of a fellow-musician I met later on Waterloo Bridge. 'It suddenly occurred to me,' he said, 'that there were three thousand of us sitting there watching a man with a small beard hit a small bell with a small stick.'

BRUBECK 1961
It may at first sight appear wildly incongruous for a group as esoteric as the Dave Brubeck Quartet to appear at the Victoria Palace, home of the ribaldries of the Crazy Gang. But in fact the Brubeck group is not above a few ribaldries of its own, like protracted quotes from 'Muskrat Ramble' in the middle of 'Tangerine'. There is no jazz attraction of any kind in the world to challenge the mass appeal of Brubeck, whose third British tour is drawing capacity houses every night. And neither is there any jazz attraction of any kind in the world whose musical quality is so charitably assessed by the public.

At the Victoria Palace Brubeck ran through a repertoire

no different in character from what we have been led to expect. But what is more important, he seems to have gained not at all in subtlety as a soloist, and it seems unlikely now that he ever will. There is about his playing a certain ineptitude of phrase which is really astonishing in one so highly regarded, and, most significantly, it is an ineptitude which one usually finds in musicians whose hearts are not really in jazz at all, but in a more formal world of musical endeavour.

But it is Brubeck's lack of judgement which will damn him in the eyes of the historians. He seems unable to distinguish between triteness and profundity, and has not shed his trick of repeating the same rhythmic phrase over an interminable number of bars, the effect of which is rather like that of being told the punch line to a joke twenty times over. Robert Benchley used to have a theory that there was no word in any language which could not be reduced to gibberish if you repeated it enough times, and some of Brubeck's improvisations seem to bear this out.

What makes the quartet worth listening to is the fragile beauty of Paul Desmond's alto saxophone. Desmond is less animated than any other jazzman I can think of. The volume of his tone is negligible and its refinement almost too exquisite, but there is an undeniable wilting appeal to his solos which at inspired moments crystallises into patterns of tremulous perfection. Whether Desmond stands aloof from the other members of the quartet by accident or design I do not know, but there were times at the Victoria Palace when, as he watched one interminable drum solo by Joe Morello, and several of Brubeck's self-admiring keyboard vagaries, he seemed disenchanted by the absence of Bud Flanagan and Nervo and Knox.

The choice of material is typically Brubeckian. Any technical challenge is gleefully accepted and triumphantly conquered, not always with musically edifying results. 'Time Out', one of Desmond's compositions, has five anarchic beats to the bar instead of four conventional ones, and 'Ballad', although conventional enough rhythmically, really needs an orchestral background for full effect.

Recently the quartet demonstrated this, for 'Ballad' is really the adagio movement from 'Dialogue for Jazz Combo and Orchestra', to be found on a new album called *Bernstein plays Brubeck plays Bernstein*. The Dialogue was composed by Brubeck's brother Howard, and the gesture seems not to have been inspired entirely by the spirit of nepotism. 'Ballad' has a distinct sentimental appeal on the recording, where it is buttressed by the sumptuous textures of the New York Philharmonic, but interpreted by alto saxophone, bass, piano and drums, it is saved only by Desmond's bewitching art.

Appearing with the quartet is a local group led by an alto saxophonist very different in character from Desmond, Joe Harriott. Under normal circumstances Harriott might be expected to supply a healthy antidote to the main attraction, but unfortunately, he is currently conducting an experiment called 'free form', which consists of not acknowledging bar-lines, not acknowledging harmonic sequences and not acknowledging the existence of melody in music. It is hard to believe that a jazz musician as accomplished as he cannot perceive the difference between free form and no form at all.

1962
HOW TO WRECK A GRAND PIANO
The world record for wrecking a grand piano stands at about fourteen minutes. At the Royal Festival Hall on Friday night it often looked like being lowered. Dave Brubeck, opening a new British tour with his quartet, and Stan Tracy working in the accompanying group led by Ronnie Scott, are two of the most percussive pianists in jazz, although of completely differing styles. Between them they must have tested severely the physical structure of the piano, especially Brubeck, who has lost none of his maddening zest for pounding cross-rhythms.

Since his last visit here Brubeck has recorded one or two albums suggesting a growing fondness for a more spectacular backdrop than the quartet. Perhaps because the current tour has begun within weeks of the release of Brubeck with full concert orchestra (Brandenburg Revisited) the sound of the quartet comes almost as a surprise. Almost but not quite. The repertoire remains the same as always, in style if not in content. There is the regional flavour borrowed from the latest tour, this time Japan, the same patient explanation of how difficult it is for a jazz musician to play in abstruse time signatures, the same occasional concession to the standard repertoire, this time 'Pennies From Heaven'. It is all skilled and cerebral music, but it remains one of the great miracles of popular taste that the Brubeck Quartet should ever have been taken seriously as one of the world's outstanding jazz combinations. Brubeck's piano playing is neither good enough to excite nor bad enough to amuse, and although the finesse of Joe Morello and bassist Eugene Wright is obvious enough, the end result continues to lack the warmth and melodic grace of the very best jazz.

'Koto Song', the mock Japanese piece, is short and mercifully quiet. In its effect it suggests what Brubeck might achieve were he less intent on being a big bad jazz musician. 'Take Five' was not to be avoided, and 'Eunisphere', the composition in three-four time, sounds too straightforward to need Brubeck's lengthy preamble. The most talented member of the quartet remains Paul Desmond, whose alto-saxophone playing, although as supine as ever, still achieves miracles of poise and ingenuity.

Sharing the bill with Brubeck is the Ronnie Scott Quartet, whose contribution, though limited to three pieces, adds greatly to the evening. Scott, who in the past two years has been responsible for the visits of several outstanding American saxophonists, plays the tenor well enough to stand comparison with all of them. His 'Some of my Best Friends are Blues' is a dazzling exercise in modulation, and 'What's New?' is in the classic tradition of jazz ballad playing, romantic without stooping to sentimentality. But perhaps it is indicative of jazz audiences in general that Brubeck's contribution was far more rapturously received.

1964
JAZZ-FANCIERS' IDOL

It is becoming increasingly difficult to remain detached from the hysteria which now accompanies any public appearance of the Dave Brubeck Quartet, but I will try. The entourage of fans has now been augmented by Tin Pan Alley, momentarily embarrassed by the fact that the Brubeck recording success 'Take Five', was so unexpected a conquest that printed copies have been hard to come by.

At the opening concert at the Royal Festival Hall last Saturday, the stage version of 'Take Five' lasted eighteen minutes, ten of which were taken up by a drum solo whose musical pointlessness was matched by the undiscriminating response of an ecstatic audience.

In the face of such acclaim it is strange indeed to sit there and arrive at the same conclusion one reached on the three previous Brubeck tours of this country. That conclusion is depressing. The quartet is so markedly deficient in certain essential jazz qualities that its popularity can hardly be regarded as a success for jazz at all. At its first recital the group revealed these deficiencies from the very opening bars. Had Brubeck opened with one of those devious compositions of his own, he might have tempted me to reserve judgement. On the contrary, his first tune was 'St Louis Blues', which constituted a grave affront to my sensibilities.

Brubeck himself remains apparently unaware of his own shortcomings as a jazz musician. His keyboard touch remains gauche and, what is much more alarming, apparently uncontrollable. He began 'St Louis Blues' with a pastiche of Count Basie's mannerisms of under-statement, but within two or three choruses he had been swept along by the impetus of his own headstrong muse into the routine crashing and bashing of block chords, studiously ignoring the bar lines as he did so. In his next piece, an original called 'Raggy Waltz', he blinded everyone with the science of playing a solo in common time against a rhythmic background of waltz time, an aspect of rhythmic virtuosity having not the remotest connection with the genuine rhythmic vitality of jazz.

His partner Paul Desmond, the most musical member of the quartet, is, it seems, being worn down at last by the sameness of his musical experiences. This is his tenth year with the quartet, and he seems now to have adopted a policy of mere passive resistance. The once girlish laughter of his alto saxophone has now become an effete whimper. He remains a technician of truly marvellous assurance, but the invertebrate nature of his solos suggests not so much an inability for playing jazz as a distaste for the whole idiom.

Audiences continue to be duped by Brubeck's subtle flattery. When they applaud the trick of playing four beats a bar against a background of only three, they are applauding not only Brubeck's cleverness but their own percipience in noticing it. They enjoy being offered titles like 'Blues Rondo à la Turk', because the implication is there that they understand blues, rondos and even Turks. Brubeck appeals to the culture vulture that resides in us all, the beast in the attic of so many jazz fanciers. His quartet produces the warm glow which comes with the assurance that the better artistic things in life are after all within our scope. But to judge

Brubeck's music by the highest jazz standards is to marvel at the comparative neglect of so many more musical groups.

1965
KILLING DRAGONS WITH BRUBECK

Each time Dave Brubeck returns to Britain it is to present a programme sounding like a parody of the last one. He appears as a modest hero, bashfully slaying the dragons of rhythmic complexity before your very eyes. And he has now arrived at the stage of informing his audience beforehand of the difficulties likely to be encountered in the next piece, rather like the illusionist who tells his audience that his next trick is impossible.

Of course, a little showmanship never harmed anybody, but the anti-climax of Brubeck's music is too marked to be compensated by any ingenuities of presentation. His keyboard touch remains gauche and his jazz conception misguided, completely lacking in the inventive power and melodic fertility that distinguish the great jazz musician. In 'This Can't Be Love', Brubeck played six choruses in each of which his improvised phrase in the first four bars of the middle section of the song was identical. To know one joke is bad enough, but to insist on telling it six times in quick succession is disastrous.

The other three members of the quartet are outstanding technicians bowed under the weight of too-familiar musical approaches. Joe Morello cannot be blamed for the marathon drum-solos perpetrated on audiences, but his great technical mastery does not save him from playing at least as twice as loud as necessary in the ensemble passages, so that much of Eugene Wright's skill as a bassist is lost. Paul Desmond's alto saxophone becomes more supine as the seasons slip by. This is his eleventh year with the quartet, and he may be pardoned if the first fine careless rapture has become dissipated.

His patterns continue to reflect academic influences, but if they were expressed in any more languid a manner they would cease to be discernible altogether.

Brubeck's big effort recently has been with an extended composition called 'The Real Ambassadors', a suite with lyrics, dedicated to the proposition that jazz is America's best ambassador. It is difficult to know whose jazz Brubeck is thinking of, but the extracts from the work which he is playing on his current tour certainly raise the question, 'Ambassadors of what?'

The curtain-raisers on this tour are the Ronnie Scott Quartet, who play three pieces and then back nervously away to make way for the hero of the hour. Scott's group, though derivative, has been wise enough to choose better models than Brubeck for its inspiration. As a result its contribution has a value to the programme out of all proportion to the size of its billing, while the title Scott chooses for his originals ('I'm sick and tired of waking up tired and sick') are at least free of pretension.

1962
RATIONING THE DECIBELS
The return visit to this country of the Modern Jazz Quartet raises no new problems to be solved, attitudes to be discussed, or motives to be detected, which is in its way a kind of tribute to the constancy of the group's pianist-leader John Lewis. He is still pursuing the ideal of a concert ensemble playing as one man and yet managing to integrate into its performance structural pre-planning which does not detract from the element of improvisation.

Nobody can take any exception to those ambitions, at least not in the theory, although perhaps musicians may be pardoned for wondering why four men should want to sound like one. The structural planning is there to an irritating degree, and the improvisation is obvious to anybody who attends more than one performance of the same theme. There are indeed those who point triumphantly to the undoubted qualities of improvisation in the quartet's work and offer this as proof of jazz validity, forgetting that improvisation has always been a red herring in jazz criticism and that what really matters is not improvisation but the preservation of its spirit, which is where the quartet fails so lamentably.

I cannot help suspecting that the polysyllabic statements of the group's credo, which reappear from time to time, are so much fudge to obscure one of the primary facts of human intercourse, which is that if you speak softly enough, any number of people will maintain a deathly hush to hear what you are saying, and that if you invest the act of rationing the decibels with an aura of sepulchral doom, then people will think they are witnessing some sacred rite and forget all about their critical faculties.

How else could the jazz-lover be duped into the quartet's version of 'How High the Moon', used as a feature for the vibraharpist Milt Jackson? There is not the slightest musical justification for playing the opening and closing choruses out of tempo, and it is a gambit which maddens people who can still remember Jackson's great rhythmic strength as a soloist. In the same way the group still persists in meddling with the time values of the melody of 'It Don't Mean a Thing' in a way which reduces the rhythmic power of Ellington's piece from a throb to a hiccup.

As to his own compositions, the intervening years since his last visit have not taught Mr Lewis that there is nothing necessarily more valid artistically about Harlequin and Columbine than there is about, say, Bill Robinson or an up-town New York apartment house, and part of the repertoire this time round consists of Lewis's *Commedia dell'arte* series in its entirety. It is quite astonishing that an American jazz musician should have this almost Jamesian obsession with the cultural connotations of the Old World, an obsession which is blinding him to the fact that the most effective way to render an intensely national art internationally valid is to retain its national traits, not to dissipate them in alien cultures.

The most maddening thing of all about the Modern Jazz Quartet is the fact that its members are all superlative musicians who can individually play jazz with bone and sinew. It is the group concept to which I take exception, and so long as the word 'jazz' is retained in the billing, then presumably we must judge them by the criteria of jazz. If so, then Lewis's piano solos really do sound indifferent. At the opening concert they were quite simpletonian, and delivered with a happy innocence of their own shortcomings which I found quite disarming, so much so that I scarcely have the heart to mention names like Tatum and Wilson, Hines and Powell in the same review.

Not that a great deal of Lewis's composition does not have considerable charm, so long as one is not misled by the billing. Some of the themes from his *Commedia dell'arte* series are quite exquisite, and I found the performance of 'Pierrot' a genuine creative experience. It is indeed magnificent, but it is not jazz.

1963
BEHIND THE MJQ MIRAGE
It is ten years now since the Modern Jazz Quartet began its
march to the New Syncopated Jerusalem. If recently a large
proportion of its followers have slunk quietly off in search of
more interesting crusades, that is hardly surprising.

Jazz fanciers now realise that the promised land was a
mirage conjured up by the MJQ's pianist-leader John Lewis.
There can be no great jazz without animation, and Lewis's
distaste for dramatics in his music necessarily limits the
group's contribution, a fact more evident than ever in the
MJQ's current British tour.

The music itself is exactly the same music as on the last
tour, and the one before that, subtle to the point of paralysis,
a whispered oration in which every phrase sounds like every
other phrase. The MJQ's programme consists of about sixteen
interpretations of various themes, and were it not for the
breaks for applause, it would be difficult to know where one
mood was supposed to end and another begin.

In his attempt to drain away the Rabelaisian element in
jazz, Lewis has succeeded all too well. Unfortunately he has
thrown out the baby with the bath-water, leaving us with a
residue of tinkling affection which I find charming after ten
minutes, tiresome after twenty and excruciating over the
length of a full concert. Not even the splendid presumption
of Lewis's titles can hide this. 'Animal Dance' turns out to be
precisely the same, in mood if not in harmonic shape, as
hoary old themes like 'All Of Me' or 'Please Don't Talk
About Me'.

The pity is that the four musicians involved are all highly
talented jazzmen. One of them, Milt Jackson, is probably
something more, but record buyers learned a long time ago
that the best way of savouring Jackson's brilliant vibraharp-
playing is not with the MJQ at all, but in the albums he
occasionally makes under his own name with different
musicians. Lewis himself continues to play respectable jazz
piano *clichés* with the air of a brilliant aphorist, but he does
it with skill and delicacy, sometimes even with humour.

There was a time when to examine the content of the
group's repertoire was like a dash on roller skates through
the pantheon of Western art, Versailles and Venice one

minute, the *Commedia dell'arte* the next. But that, it seems, is all over. Nearly one-third of the MJQ's opening concert last week-end was devoted to the score of 'Porgy and Bess', nearly one-third of the remainder to conventional 12-bar themes. It is all much more bearable musically, but it is a strange ending to the quest for respectability in jazz. Gershwin and the blues. Where next? Or, as John Lewis would perhaps prefer to put it, *quo vadis?*

Saxophones

From my fourteenth to my thirty-third year there were perhaps a hundred days when I did not open a saxophone case and inhale the distinctive musk of its interior. Long before I appreciated the process, the saxophone had become an integral part of my existence, an extension of my body which I so took for granted that when inquisitive witnesses pointed to a certain key or rod, as they sometimes did, asking what service it performed, I had always to take the instrument in my hands before knowing the answer, much as an athlete has to flex his muscles to discover which of them are inclined to ripple in differing circumstances. The one occasion when I did not put a polite face on it and attempt to answer one of these queries was on the bandstand of a long-since demolished holiday camp overlooking the Solent, where a young girl asked me which hand I played the tune with.

In jazz the saxophone is unique in that it is the only instrument which, once defined, further subdivides itself. A trumpeter is a trumpeter, but an alto player is almost never a tenor player. Over the years a few gifted musicians have demonstrated mastery over two of the four standard saxophones, and at least one saxophonist, Sonny Stitt, has offered substantial proof of his mastery over three, but it is a general rule that although all saxophones are variations of each other, the alto being the baritone pitched an octave higher, the tenor being the soprano an octave lower, and so on, it is also true that each of the four subdivisions possesses such unique qualities of tone, weight, shape, pitch and timbre as to render it distinct from the others.

When I began playing the saxophone, finding the weight of the tenor a serious distraction, I learned instead for a while on a curved soprano, a curio of great charm which looked rather like an outsize meerschaum pipe and whose resemblance to the armour of Achilles was explained by the accident of its once having been blown by Sidney Bechet. Later I graduated to a silver-plated Martin tenor, and still later, in the spring of 1949, to a gold-plated Conn tenor, whose acquirement has remained one of the watersheds of my life. The power of its resonance and the ease with which its keys responded to the touch, commended themselves to me so irresistibly that to this day I have retained my affection for that instrument, never having considered exchanging it either for money or another saxophone, because I know that whatever the outcome of such a transaction, I should have struck a bad bargain, I took it on a gig with me one Saturday night, before I had even signed the Hire Purchase agreement or paid the first instalment, blew a chorus on it of 'Slow Boat to China' and knew I must have it, even though I had not the remotest idea where the money was coming from. Years later there was a long professional interlude when I masqueraded as a baritone saxophonist, but as I had neither much affection nor much aptitude for that most cumbersome of instruments, I continued to regard myself as a tenor saxophonist, which, in defiance of the musical evidence, I still do.

The following reviews of saxophonists were all outcomes of nights spent at Ronnie Scott's Club, an establishment which, being administered by a man who was himself a gifted saxophonist, tended, especially in its early days, to concentrate on masters of that instrument in preference to masters of any other. In the days when I had been one of his partners in a co-operative orchestral venture, I had come to know Scott as a man whose love of and curiosity about the saxophone was limitless. He had a much wider knowledge of past saxophone styles than most of his contemporaries in the modern movement, and once in a hotel bedroom somewhere between Penzance and Inverness, when I played him an old Lester Young recording, he shook his head in admiration of Young's playing, and then gave it the highest praise he could think of, 'Nothing fancy. Just notes.' And two years later, when we were in New York, he came bursting into my room with the news that he had just heard the greatest saxophone player in the world and that I must drop everything and go and hear for myself. I did drop everything and did go and hear for myself. The player was Sonny Stitt, and I have been grateful to Scott ever since for dragging me out of that hotel room.

Under such circumstances, it was hardly surprising that

Scott, when at last he realised an old ambition and became
the proprietor of his own club, should indulge his taste for
the great saxophone masters, or that people like myself
should respond so delightedly. When he first began import-
ing American guest musicians, Scott stuck exclusively to
saxophonists, for which policy he was, incredibly, attacked
by some people who wanted a more varied bill of fare. Scott,
as is his habit in such situations, took no notice, and went
on pleasing himself and all the other saxophonists who
approved of his policy. For us the situation was heaven-sent.
Time after time Scott trotted out figures from our legendary
past, personalities with whom I had first become acquainted
through the remote contact of the occasional recording, artists
whose findings had become so integral a part of my mental
furniture that to discover at this late stage that they were
after all not disembodied sounds but real men was a shock
whose delights did not always outweigh the disappointments.

The one great problem posed by the succession of saxophone virtuosi was that of passing time. While men like Getz
and Sims were still in their prime, others were not, and the
problem was typified by the giant shadow of Coleman
Hawkins. For me, or Scott, or any other member of our
generation, to have the effrontery to pick faults with Coleman Hawkins, was a situation too absurd to contemplate.
In so far as Hawkins had virtually invented tenor saxophone
playing as a civilised pursuit, there was a sense in which he
could therefore be said to have invented musicians like Scott,
myself and the whole of our generation. Had it not been for
Hawkins there would have existed no saxophone traditon
to tempt us into the jazz life in the first place, so when we
came flocking to see this man, we did so with a very special
affection. On the other hand, the very fact that we understood so thoroughly and revered so deeply the Hawkins
masterpieces of the past, meant that we were well aware that
we were extremely unlikely to hear any further masterpieces
in the future. Hawkins inevitably had declined, and it would
have been not only dishonest of us to ignore the fact, but
also disloyal to the original masterpieces, whose currency
could only be debased if we went around insisting, as some
people did, that Hawkins still played as well as ever. But
what of that vast credit balance in Hawkins's aesthetic
account? How could anyone ignore that? In reviewing him I
was understandably eager to find some evidence of the old
flair. To my immense relief I found it, if only in a few

scattered instances, and was happy to say so.

The night when I found myself sitting in judgement on Hawkins was perhaps the moment when I felt the fundamental absurdity of my position more acutely than at any other. This was Coleman Hawkins, who had flattened my adolescent sensibilities with the colossal panache of his recordings of 'Stardust', 'Out of Nowhere', 'When Day is Done', 'The Day You Came Along', 'Honeysuckle Rose'. His Master's Voice. Five shillings and fourpence halfpenny. A red label. Steel needles and a hand-winder gramophone. From Hawkins as much as from anybody with the possible exception of Lester Young, I had acquired all of the grammar and the vocabulary of jazz as I was ever likely to possess. I had sat at his feet; how could I now sit on his head?

It was a problem duplicated each time one of the giants turned up on Scott's bandstand. There was Getz, whose brief but beautiful solo in Woody Herman's 'Summer Sequence' I had conned by rote in 1948, only to be frustrated in my attempts to play it because none of the rhythm sections of my apprentice days knew the harmonies of the theme; Sims, whose teenaged playing in 'Four Brothers' had first suggested to me that there might just conceivably be others beside myself who had heard of Lester Young; Konitz, one of whose transcribed solos I had tried to play one afternoon in unison with an alto saxophonist of my acquaintance, succeeding only in evoking the wrath of his mother, who couldn't stand the noise. And so it always was. Each of these saxophonists was an instalment in my own musical biography, which made my critical obligations at once easier and yet very much harder.

On the night Hawkins opened at Scott's, I suddenly remembered an afternoon ten years before, at the holiday camp by the Solent. It was a period when for the first time I was beginning to have grave doubts about my desire to go on being a professional musician, a misgiving which was only complicated by the fact that in all my working life I had never been anything else. The prospects of blowing a baritone in a section until I was eligible for a pension had so horrified me earlier that year that I had retreated to this camp where I could at least return to my old friend the Conn tenor, and give myself time to think. One day after lunch, taking a breather while practising on the deserted bandstand, I began idly turning over the sheets at the back of my looseleaf folder of orchestral parts. This was the section of the book we never ever referred to while playing for the customers, and I was not surprised to see that it consisted of last season's hits, discarded novelty pieces, vocal medleys, and the rest of the waste material which always accumulates in every folder of every musician in every professional orchestra in the world.

Many of the printed parts had been defaced in the usual obscene style. There were phone numbers, doodles, limericks, addresses, scribbled in the contrasting hands of all the past incumbents of my job. And there, right at the back, folded inside a printed piano copy of a long-forgotten song called 'The Maharajah of Mogador', was a double sheet of manuscript covered in small, neatly-inscribed notes. Bored with the tedium of scale practice, and disenchanted long ago with the holiday camp repertoire, I began to study the notations before me. Silently I fingered the keys of the Conn, and gradually began to puff air down the dusty burnished tunnel of its bore. What I had stumbled upon was something which I would have considered beyond price in my teens, a transcription of Hawkins' 'Body and Soul', the most famous recorded saxophone solo of all time, and a mark for all future generations of saxophonists to aim at. I was, of course, unable to play the complete solo through, and was consoled in my ineptitude by the recollection of the story, probably not apocryphal, that Hawkins himself had once denied his own ability to play it if confronted by it in the manuscript form I had discovered in this least likely of places. For the rest of the afternoon I explored that remarkable solo, playing such extracts from it as my technique allowed me, reacquainting myself with the contours of a masterpiece I had first encountered at sixteen and been overawed by ever since.

It was a purely fortuitous encounter, and it came at a moment when it was especially reassuring to me to be reminded that my adolescent sensibilities had responded so promptly to so outstanding a work. Eventually I reached a point where neither my fingers nor my brain could follow where Hawkins had been, so I replaced the sheet of music at the back of the folder and never referred to it again. While I was remembering all this, Hawkins shambled on to the bandstand at Scott's and began tuning up. And yet from time to time I have come across people who have demanded some kind of idealised purple patch which they describe as objective criticism.

LUCKY THOMPSON 1964
WOOING THE SOPRANO

Lucky Thompson's nightly performance at Ronnie Scott's Club must be causing considerable surprise among those who flattered themselves they were familiar with his saxophone style through his recordings.

For the past ten years Thompson has maintained a reputation for romantic improvisation almost too rich in harmonic ingenuity. His playing incorporated so many chord movements that there were times when his preoccupation with arpeggios caused his melodic patterns to be stilted. He was like a man with his nose so close to the map that he did not always observe the beauties of the countryside.

But he has now appeared in London playing in a style much closer to that of the general modernist movement. The effect is altogether less formal and in a way disappointing. Whatever his old shortcomings, Thompson was a highly cultured musician. At the moment his simulation of earthier effects is well done, technically dazzling, but less personal. There are a dozen saxophonists who do exactly the same kind of thing.

Thompson, in fact, is a very odd case, a musician with all the harmonic equipment of a modernist, but whose whole aesthetic is founded on the Swing Age precepts of Coleman Hawkins. It might be unfortunate if he merged into the general anonymity of modern saxophone playing, for although he is clever enough to be able to conform to fashion, he is also a gifted enough stylist in his own right to keep his own counsel.

His current obsession with the soprano saxophone is another indication that he is following trends. After long neglect, the soprano is being courted once more, and Thompson certainly plays this difficult instrument better than the spearhead of the revival, John Coltrane. But both Thompson and Coltrane are tenor players, and to transfer their mannerisms from the tenor to the soprano would be fatal.

The soprano is different, not in degree, but in kind, from the rest of the saxophone family. Having hardly any tonal contrast between its upper and lower registers, it demands a bold, simple style which strides across the complete range of the instrument within a single phrase; otherwise everything is going to seem to revolve around a very narrow axis, which is what happens with Thompson at times. It is significant that Sidney Bechet, the only major soprano saxophonist in jazz history, was extremely partial to arpeggios which spanned the entire range of the instrument, and never played any of the larger saxophones.

In the last reckoning Thompson is a musician's musician by virtue of his astonishing technique. Whether playing hysterically, as in 'Cherokee', or funereally, as in 'Lover Man', his mastery of all technical problems is so complete that it is apt to blind one to his occasional lack of melody. There are moments when he seems deliberately to have placed technical considerations before all else. If this is true, then Thompson is heading for the same ambush that the entire current generation of modernists tumbled into.

LEE KONITZ 1966

The Lee Konitz of fond memory was an alto saxophonist whose one heroic achievement was to retain his own identity at a time, fifteen years ago, when all others were trying to pass themselves off as Charlie Parker. The Lee Konitz currently appearing at Ronnie Scott's is undoubtedly the same man. He looks like his photographs and plays the same instrument. But if jazzmen worked from behind a screen nobody would think so.

Today he is just one of many players of his generation baffled by the turn that jazz improvisation has taken, feeling a duty to move with the times and sacrificing his own originality in the process.

The Konitz of 1966 sounds a confused artist. His thoughts no longer flow. If the neologisms of younger men are ugly, he still feels obliged to echo them. The strength of musical will which enabled him to resist the siren song of Parker's style has wilted in the face of newer fashions, so that his solos are disjointed affairs where the old coherence peeps through for a few bars before being swamped by groping and uncertainty.

One of jazz's master technicians, Konitz, today, instead of struggling to express his own thoughts struggles to express other people's, and the result is a moving demonstration of the truth about jazz that each player possesses only one personality and therefore only one style, and that to attempt to change it is commendable but from the musical view nearly always fatal.

For those of us raised on his wonderful facility of the old days, it is a shattering experience to hear him play an old standard like 'Indiana' and drown himself in the deep waters of an impossibly fast tempo, harder still to hear him tackle the beautiful harmonies of 'Round Midnight' and appear to be unfamiliar with the possibilities of his instrument.

Perhaps he is a player whose standard of performance fluctuates violently from night to night. Certainly his more recent recordings give no hint of the confusion which appears to be raging in his mind in London.

After Konitz, the air is cleared at Scott's by the surface innocence of Blossom Dearie's singing. After four bars the inclination is to laugh. But slowly Miss Dearie's quiet persistence takes over, her exquisite sense of timing begins to register, and the childlike demeanour is seen to be a mere front for a highly sophisticated style. She is also a moderate pianist who accompanies herself, wandering in a dreamlike state through an intelligently selected programme which reaches its climax with the deadly naïveté of 'When in Rome'. A sense of humour in a jazz singer is a rare gift and Blossom Dearie has it.

In the meantime local audiences are trying to gather their wits after the lightning tour of the Duke Ellington Orchestra. The Duke was no sooner in the country than he was out of it again, having given us no more than a tantalising taste of what he could do. His concert partnership with Ella Fitzgerald may have been a case of two for the price of one. On the other hand it was also a case of half a loaf from each artist, which is better than none but hardly satisfactory to devoted Ellingtonians, who rightly support each Ellington tour as though it might be the last.

The concert alliance with Ella really does no more than underline the problem which has aways worried supporters of the Ellington concerts. What programme should the Duke play? Should he present Ellington the composer by rendering some of his longer suites? Or should he show off the individual brilliancies of his musicians? It is a false choice, because with a little skilful programming he could do both at once. On the current tour, restricted to half his normal playing time, Ellington opts for the soloists at the expense of the composer, and although they put on a dazzling show, they cannot quite give us the very best of Ellington.

ROLAND KIRK 1968

In the past, general impressions of Roland Kirk have been that his extraordinary multi-instrumental sleight of hand obscures a fine orthodox jazz talent. His latest performances at Ronnie Scott's Club suggest that the proposition should now be reversed, and that it is the jazz talent which is obscuring the trickery.

A man who can snort passable solos by thrusting a specially constructed flute up his nostrils, who builds his own saxophones and then plays three of them at the same time, who disturbs the flow of his own improvisations by making whooping noises on a hunting whistle, is not quite the artist to endear himself to purists. And yet there is no question that behind his amazing contrivance, half-buried under elastic bands and Heath Robinson instruments, lies an acute jazz brain.

What seems to be happening to Kirk is that in his quite genuine attempts to entertain his audiences, coherence is occasionally being sacrificed to effect. If jazz is losing one of its most promising younger men, which looks likely, then it is gaining the first purely musical clown in its history. Past jokers like Fats Waller and Louis Armstrong were serious enough while actually playing, but Kirk's solos are in themselves funny. Interludes of beautiful lucidity on the tenor saxophone, the only orthodox instrument in the Kirk armoury, are interspersed with noises so peculiar that it is hard to define them.

His latest trick is to sing through the mouthpiece at the same time as he is blowing through it, so that one is never quite sure that what is coming out is a speech or a solo. In 'My Ship', played on the flute, the long introduction consists of a series of London dock noises which perhaps take Kurt Weill's title a little too literally. And yet when Kirk gets down to the meat of the song, he plays with an enviable flair.

Possibly he will be the man to rescue jazz from its most threatening peril, the isolation from audiences. At the climax of his evenings, he passes among the crowd with penny whistles, which he then manages to assimilate into his own performance. By making every jazz fan his own soloist in this way, Kirk brings home to the non-player a taste of the thrill of music-making as nobody else has ever done.

The doubt left is how far the joke is meant to be taken. When he plays an absurd cod version of a 1920s tear-jerker, the audience dutifully sees the joke and laughs knowingly. It is perhaps surprising that they do not laugh a little sooner, when Kirk bursts into his long flurries of notes and special effects which are not so much sound as noise.

Kirk is supported, if such a thing is possible, by a girl called Norma Winstone, whose evident unfamiliarity with the intense atmosphere of a jazz club has unnerved her. The appearance of any new girl singer is rare enough, but when she is, in the words of the proprietor, 'Not only promising, but British,' the debut becomes unique.

The critics who have been pummelling Miss Winstone have shown an indecent haste to point out that her performance is displeasing without saying why. Briefly, she suffers from a surfeit of ambition.

Her attempt to remould every song she sings while contriving to make the new melody fit the syllables of the lyric, is a task so terrifying that it is doubtful if even Billie Holiday herself could have pulled it off.

Miss Winstone has a good idea of jazz inflection and a useful range. If she chose a more sympathetic programme and let the tune do part of the work, she might yet prove the critics wrong.

ZOOT AND AL 1965

No sooner has Ben Webster vacated the stand at Ronnie Scott's Club than Zoot Sims and Al Cohn move in, reminding us that there are more ways than one of blowing a tenor saxophone. Webster belongs to the old school, the one so heavily influenced by the hot romanticism of Coleman Hawkins. Sims and Cohn, two of the most gifted of the promising young lads of twenty years ago, are so obviously derivative of Lester Young that it is no wonder that they sound like identical twins.

And yet they are not quite identical. Although they both think in terms of Young's honking tone, and break down a melody in the same way, they retain individual musical personalities.

Cohn tries for a heavyweight tone and gets it. By modern standards his harmonic approach is naïve, strange in a man whose instrumental ability in the last few years has been overshadowed by the brilliance of his work as composer and orchestrator. The real trouble here is the company he keeps. Put him up by himself and he sounds as lively a saxophonist as anyone could wish for. But Cohn rarely does play by himself these days. His partnership with Zoot Sims has lasted many years, ever since the historic Woody Herman band of the late 1940s, and this means that a review of Cohn usually ends up as an appreciation of his partner.

Sims, it seems to me, is one of the great jazz musicians of his era. His style can only be described as beautiful. He is one of the least cluttered soloists alive, every note being executed in a bold, clear tone, and every phrase being utterly right in its context. Above all, there is the rhythmic exhilaration of his playing.

Today it is possible, because of the abstruse harmonic findings of modernists, to get a huge reputation without once sounding as though playing jazz is an enjoyable business. The true test of a soloist is the extent to which he would have survived in earlier periods of the music's history, and listening to Sims fly through his solos, one guesses that he would have thrived at any time in the last forty years. He is that rare bird, the jazz natural, the playing fool, whose windy tone and facile fingers have somehow elevated a copyist into a great original.

What does Sims get out of the collaboration with Cohn? The answer is thought and cunning, an organising mind. Most of the repertoire in the Sims-Cohn act consists of originals composed by Cohn, who has arranged them for two instrumental voices, sometimes using simple unison, occasionally fanning out into pleasing two-part harmony. And, not surprisingly, the kind of material Cohn produces is tailor-made for the jazz style of the two men. It moves in predictable patterns; it glances now and then in the direction of Charlie Parker, but most of the time it is rooted in the old conventions of the Swing Age. Today a judgement like that is more and more becoming a compliment.

GETZ 1969
No matter how trying his existence, the professional critic has one consolation, which is that the racing form of the great soloists almost never undergoes any dramatic transformation. In the whole history of jazz it is hard to find a

single goose that changed overnight into a swan, and the reverse process always takes place with the comforting inevitability of gradualness.

This is why, in the past few days at Ronnie Scott's, the slaughter has been truly terrible. Connoisseurs have been leaving the premises in dazed distress. We have all been witnessing the one spectacle we thought was utterly beyond the bounds of possibility, Stan Getz playing the tenor saxophone untidily.

For many years now Getz has been recognised as the most immaculate of all the great players, a supreme artist whose whole approach rests on the basis of an infallible technique and a melodic coherence that has been the wonder of the jazz-world. Nobody who witnessed it has ever forgotten the staggering brilliance of his season here five years ago, and none of his recordings since has given the slightest hint of any decline.

But the first week of his current season has been a week of confusion, of squeaks and honks, long pauses between phrases, uncertainty of direction in even the most familiar themes, and a general indifference to the distress these solecisms were causing. It is one of the most astonishing reversals of form by an American master that this country has ever witnessed.

There are, apparently, some rational explanations. Getz appears to have arrived here very short of match practice, having been parted from his saxophone for at least a month. There has also been some trouble in the rhythm section, whose drummer was changed after four nights. Even so, it has been a great shock to hear the finest tenor saxophonist of the last twenty years blowing themes like 'Con Alma', and 'Desafinado' as though he had never heard of them before, and an even greater one eavesdropping on his attempts to control a new instrument, the soprano saxophone, just about the most difficult instrument to master in the whole range of jazz.

I doubt very much whether all this signifies the permanent decline of Getz. Even in his worst moments this week there have been flashes of the old control. He has sounded not like a poor player but like a great one in momentary crisis. The real trouble is that he has set such impossible standards in the past that anything less than utter mastery comes as a slap in the face.

Probably by the end of the month he will have recovered all his marvellous aplomb. It may even turn out to be a profound experience watching him climb back up the mountain during his season. But for the moment he has mislaid those remarkable gifts.

GETZ 1969, SECOND THOUGHTS

After witnessing Stan Getz's troubled state when he opened his season at Ronnie Scott's a fortnight ago, it was impossible not to go back again to see how this remarkable musician's pursuit of his own composure was progressing. Not surprisingly, it is progressing very well.

Already the ballad playing is being executed with the old sweetness and control. And there are clear signs that his ability to coin phrases of melodic beauty was not lost when he arrived here, but only mislaid. He is, after all, one of the greatest improvisers ever, and it is only natural that he should blow his way out of a bad patch without wasting too much time.

But what is far more interesting than his reassertion of the old mastery is the indication that radical changes are taking place in his basic approach to jazz. It now becomes apparent that what sounded like a confusion two weeks ago was not due entirely to uncertainty of touch. Not only his lip and fingers were hesitant, but his mind also.

Getz has always been an evolving player. Indeed his advance from the coy, slightly whimsical virtuosity of the early 1950s to the sinuous muscularity of ten years later has been one of the deepest pleasures that jazz has known in this generation. There now appears to be a further change on the way, and a very profound one. To be concise, Getz is attempting to reshape his whole style. The jagged phrases and the eccentric intervals indicate that he has taken due note of the cavortings of the *avant garde* and is making a serious attempt to synthesise some of its more relevant findings into his own work.

No jazz musicians of Getz's classical attitudes has ever succeeded in performing this difficult trick so far, although John Coltrane died two years ago at a vital stage in the process. But Getz is one of the most highly intelligent as well as one of the most gifted natural musicians in jazz, and the fact that his curiosity has once again been aroused is a healthy sign. In the meantime, his quartet, strengthened by the acquisition of the drummer Jack de Johnette, is already progressing towards the point where it will soon sound like one man with eight hands instead of four with one and a half.

ZOOT 1969
THE SWEET SIMS WAY

Zoot Sims, currently appearing at Ronnie Scott's, is going to restore quite a few battered faiths before he goes home again. Jazz has been sliding into anarchy for so long now, and at such a pace, that even in provincial outposts of musical sensibility, like New York, commentators are beginning to wonder whether shrinking audiences, shrinking catalogues and the stampede by so many opportunists towards the flesh-pots of Pop, all add up to proof that jazz is after all a finite art, now approaching its extreme limits.

In the middle of all this gloom and despondency Zoot Sims appears and plays as though this were the golden age. Of course Sims has always been a remarkable player, ever since he came out of the Woody Herman band more than twenty years ago, remarkable for the complete lack of affectation in his music, the resilience of his style and the uncanny relaxation with which he expressed it. All these qualities have been well enough known to jazz fans for many years now, and that is the whole point. Such qualities decay all too quickly, but Sims has somehow managed to hang on to all of them.

In the present climate, his presence is far more important than ever before. Most of his generation lost their nerve years ago and went galloping off in the wake of younger men who themselves had very little idea where they were going. Sims, ignoring the infantile dialectics of the jazz theorists who have confused freedom with anarchy, has gone his own sweet way, with marvellous results.

Whether playing standards like 'Too Close For Comfort' and 'I Hear a Rhapsody' or a down-to-earth blues, Sims reminds us of the almost tactile quality of great saxophone playing. At 43 he is one of the great jazz players of the world, and there is a moral in it all, expressed by Alan Branscombe, the pianist in the excellent British trio which accompanies him. Recovering from the pleasant shock of playing with a soloist who still respects harmonic logic and tonal beauty, Branscombe admitted the strangeness of encountering such old-fashioned virtues and remarked that the only sensible course for any jazz musician is to admit that he is what he is and play accordingly.

Zoot Sims has always done this, and the expansiveness, the maturity, the joy in craftsmanship, the sheer unpretentiousness of his playing, suggests that most of the freakers-out of the *avant-garde* are not trail blazers at all, but a bunch of aspiring Zoots who never made it.

HAWK 1968

If tomorrow Shakespeare were to turn up in a state of advanced decrepitude with a mediocre play under his arm, where would be the critic to attempt a dispassionate assessment? Because jazz history has been telescoped into a brief fifty-year period, that is precisely the dilemma awaiting those who go to Ronnie Scott's Club in London this month to hear Coleman Hawkins playing the tenor saxophone.

Hawkins was the first man ever to give the instrument any kind of coherence. Before he arrived, saxophones were a vaudeville joke; after he had done his work they were recognised as machines which could, in the right hands, create music of sumptuous beauty. All jazz criticism today is based on the standards of a handful of men like him, and even if a few players like Charlie Parker and Lester Young have managed to survive the comparison, Hawkins still stands first because it was he who started the whole business. Without him there would have been no saxophone tradition in jazz at all.

But Hawkins today is long past his prime, and not even the vast fund of good will that has accumulated over the years on his behalf can hide the fact. Admittedly, some people are so delighted that at 64 he is still playing at all that they go completely wild and insist that the old man is as good as ever. This is not only to over-rate his current playing, but to place his earlier masterpieces in an unflattering light.

In the 1940s there was no tenor player who could live with him. The greatest improviser at slow tempo of his generation, Hawkins also possessed the most remarkable sense of form ever heard in jazz, so that instinctively he could make a few random choruses grow into a single unified statement. There was no harmonic subtlety he could not grasp and no technical problem he could not cope with.

The contrast between then and now is underlined by the way he tackles 'Sweet Georgia Brown' at Scott's Club. The speed of the piece seems to cause him problems, and he is struggling so hard to keep up that there is no time left for invention. Exactly thirty years ago in Paris, Hawkins recorded this same theme there with a brilliance that was an inspiration to thousands of other jazz musicians. In the same way, his present version of 'Moonglow' suffers largely because of the great achievements of the past which overshadow it. Here is a leisurely tempo Hawkins can settle into without strain, but although the old harmonic sense still flickers into life, the melodic stream has dried up.

And yet Hawkins today, frail in body as well as in spirit, retains the courage of a lion. This has always been one of the most admirable things about him as an artist. When the post-war modernists first arrived breathing fire, almost alone of the established masters he fraternised with them, studied their methods and even gave them jobs. In this way he probably prolonged his life as an influential soloist by at least ten years, although it was not the instinct of self-preservation which impelled him so much as his burning curiosity about music. And he remains curious to the end.

At Scott's he plays 'September Song' out of tempo and unaccompanied: no rhythmic section to lean on, no pleasant piano chords to hide behind. It is a stroke of great defiance, because the unaccompanied saxophone solo is the cruellest test of all, invented by Hawkins himself half a lifetime ago. And yet in 'September Song' he produces his best playing of the evening.

Gruff as the tone is, long as the pauses are betwen phrases, a vast map of Kurt Weill's harmonies is unfolded and transformed into a landscape by the innate romanticism of the soloist's style. It may be jazz played from memory, but at least Hawkins is remembering his own work and not other people's.

GETZ 1971

Jazz people are just as susceptible as anybody else to the ancient fraud that the golden age ended the day before yesterday, and will therefore be stupefied by what they find if they take the trouble to drop in at Ronnie Scott's club between now and next Sunday night.

Having dropped in, they will certainly be in no great hurry to drop out again, because they will have the privilege of hearing not just one of the great jazz masters of all time, but a jazz master who is not long in the tooth and style. It is doubtful if Stan Getz has ever player better in his life. When we consider this in the light of his past achievements it becomes a little clearer what kind of jazz is being created in London at this moment.

Getz's return to the staggering form of a few years ago is one of the best things that could have happened to jazz. On his last two visits here he showed – in 1969 – a natural but misguided interest in *avant-garde* tricks and, in 1970, how impossible it is for a saxophonist to be relaxed while suffering from the handicap of broken bones. Getz, however, has always had a conception of himself as romantic as the music he plays, and his spectacular efforts over the past year to retain full physical fitness have certainly paid some beautiful dividends. He goes for twenty-minute runs each morning, which is nothing compared to the distance he travels each night on the bandstand at Scott's.

To analyse his current playing is a simple task and a pleasurable one. His tone is the most musical any saxophonist has produced for at least thirty years, the old slightly cloying sweetness having matured into something still sweet but more resilient. His technique is quite awe-inspiring, and it perhaps needs to be pointed out that technique includes control of dynamics as well as playing lots of notes quickly. In 'I Remember Clifford', Getz orchestrates his own solo with the subtlest gradations of volume, producing an effect so mesmeric that all the current dialectical troubles of jazz fall away and are forgotten.

As for what he plays, his melodic gift remains as prodigious as ever. It so happens that having spent the last two or three years tinkering with the exquisite engine of his own style, he has now succeeded in putting all the pieces together again, supported by a French rhythm section whose members are not only worthy accompanists, but are also providing him with a great many excellent compositions.

Getz's genius has flowered again at a particularly significant moment in jazz development, when form is laughed at and any kind of creative discipline is suspected of being passionless. Not surprisingly, he believes that the soloist should calculate the odds most carefully before committing himself to any radical change in approach. Whatever his theories are worth – and he is the shrewdest of musical thinkers – there is no question of his executive greatness. In being graced by so consummate a musician, jazz in 1971 is perhaps luckier than it deserves.

GETZ 1962
BACK TO THE BOSSA NOVA

The welcome reappearance of the early bossa nova albums confirms the view that while the music industry spent the 1960s being distracted by loud noises from the nursery, the real innovations in the composition and treatment of popular songs were taking place elsewhere.

At the time, the bossa nova irruption seemed to consist merely of 'Desafinado', 'The Girl from Ipanema', and one or two other items on Stan Getz's amazing first bossa nova album, *Jazz Samba*. It gradually became apparent that these tunes were no more than the tip of the iceberg, and that Getz had almost accidentally revealed to the world at least two song writers of major stature, Antonio Carlos Jobin and João Gilberto. Soon a third writer, Luis Bonfá, joined them, until by the middle of the 1960s it was obvious that the Brazilian songwriters comprised the first significant wave of new talent since the European immigrant school of fifty years before.

From the purist jazz standpoint, the novelty of bossa nova wore itself out very quickly, and the process can be followed in the current flood of reissues. 'Jazz Samba' was, of course, one of the great recordings of its generation, the album which put Getz's standing as an original beyond argument. With its successor, *Jazz Sambo Encore,* conventions were already being established, and there was a general tendency to respect the written melody rather more than before. Even so, in 'Um Abraço no Getz' the jazz was as magnificent as ever, while in 'Insensatez', the frankly sentimental lyricism of Jobim's ballad-writing was perfectly expressed by Getz, who has never been above a bit of frankly sentimental lyricism himself.

In 1963 Getz and Jobim joined forces with the guitarist João Gilberto to record *Getz-Gilberto* and a year later the same team's concert at Carnegie Hall was recorded and issued as *Getz-Gilberto No 2.* By now bossa nova was obeying the law of diminishing returns. The occasional item still established itself as a minor hit, but what was more interesting, and remains so today, is that Jobim and Gilberto represent a whole school of writers whose freshness and melodic richness have revitalised the tired form of the standard song.

Whether the bossa nova should really have been the bombshell it was is an awkward question. Bonfá and Jobim had already shown their class when they collaborated on the score for 'Black Orpheus', but there had been a much earlier and much more pointed hint. In 'Jazz Samba' the last of the eight tracks is one of the most beautiful of all the bossa nova melodies, 'Baia'. Composed by one Barroso, it had been a minor hit a generation earlier when it appeared in a Walt Disney film, a straw in the wind which nobody noticed for twenty years.

Cult and Culture

Mine was the generation which saw jazz grow from a cultural backwater in which the train-spotting tiddlers of the discographies and the matrix numbers sported happily to the edification of each other and the enlightenment of absolutely nobody else, into a great flourishing cultural stock exchange where a Black Friday could result in the dramatic fall in this or that musician's market value, or a buoyant period could see vastly inflated reputations go soaring. An example of both of these phenomena is the fact that for a long period in the 1950s, Lee Konitz was being quoted at a far higher figure than Johnny Hodges, Chet Baker than Clark Terry, Herbie Mann than Coleman Hawkins. Of all these fluctuations and the factors which brought them about, the one sure way for a musician to guarantee the improvement of his own position was to die. The increase in prestige which always followed this event was enormous, but it must be understood that it was a manipulative device which could hardly be used more than once.

The increasing cultural significance of jazz culminated finally in the most remarkable scenes of critical carnage, what with the intervention of Norman Mailer with his Hip-Square league tables, and the amazing discovery of Mr L. P. Hartley who, in a 1970 anthology called 'Promise of Greatness', finally solved the problem which had been puzzling the whole world for the last fifty years, when he announced that jazz had been the cause of the First World War. These vast advances of jazz on the cultural front meant that many thousands of well-intentioned social climbers were left stranded on the shores of ambition without so much as a cockleshell of knowledge to take them out on to the high seas of pretension. The following two pieces were intended as a kind of consumer guide for all would-be jazzosophers, who, having digested the contents of the two essays which follow, would be relieved of the need to listen to the actual music at all.

The absolute success of the two pieces in this regard explains the fall of jazz album sales in the last few years. The backwater looms once more.

THE NAME DROPPERS

So far as the Gentle Art of Namedropping is concerned, the jazz world turns out, as usual, to be a very special case indeed. The difficulty is a very serious one, and is summed up with admirable precision in an exchange of dialogue in an early Lenny Bruce recording. An interviewer is asking an *avant-garde* horn player how he feels about his music . . .

Interviewer: 'Now tell me, what do you think about Art?'
Hippy Hornist: 'I think Art blows the most, man.'

Feeble as it may be, Bruce's joke teaches one daunting lesson, which is that inside the jazz world there are no second names. By the very act of mentioning a surname the aspiring namedropper is rendering his own technique totally ineffective. In jazz the name you drop is usually the baptismal one, often the acquired one, never the real one. So far as the professional hippie is concerned, Bruce's interviewer could conceivably have been referring to Art Tatum, Art Blakey, Art Farmer, Art Hodes, Art Ellefson, or even Artie Shaw, but never by the remotest stretch of the imagination to art itself.

This simple fact explains why, when the outsider eavesdrops on an exchange of opinions between insiders, sanity seems to dissolve at an alarming rate –

'Ya dig Zoot?'

'It's Stan for me, baby.'

'But that's all Prez and water.'

'That's cool. But Bean's the father.'

'What's Bean to do with Stan, baby? It's like Bird and Rabbit taking fours.'

'You listen to Paul and then you wouldn't think so.'

The fact that there is much critical shrewdness in that kind of exchange is beside the point. Critical shrewdness is not the object of the exercise. Our two connoisseurs are demonstrating, not their ability to analyse style, but their long familiarity with the elusive art of latching on to the litany, a litany incidentally, which happens to possess at least as much poetic content as Joyce's *Anna Livia Plurabelle*. The aspiring jazz namedropper has been trying without success for years to devise a mnemonic to cover Stomp, Chuck, Stump, Chick, Tick, Scrap, Snub, Spoon, Stuff, Shake, Snurps, Tut, Chippie, Smokey, Zutty and Zinkie. Even the most subtle performer can stumble over the fine lines which separate Satchelmouth from Gatemouth, Cleanhead from Fathead, Peewee from Peanuts. Neither is there any skirting these issues, because many of these oddly-named gentlemen are vital figures in the development of the music. Had Shaw's Dubedat been a jazzman instead of a painter, his dying speech might have read, 'I believe in Duke, Pops and Diz, in the might of Cannonball, the mystery of Jelly Roll, the redemption of all things by Cow-Cow everlasting and the message of Artie that has made these hands blessed.' And hearing that speech, every namedropper in the jazz world would be able to tick off each label as it came, lamenting as he did so the sad omission of Chu, Nosey, Stovepipe, Boots, Buster and Smack.

Culturally of course, this kind of thing has proved disastrous for the sociological standing of jazz. The names sound so undignified that the layman may perhaps be pardoned for assuming that the music does too. There was even a sporadic attempt by the namedroppers of a generation ago to recover a hopeless situation by reverting back to surnames. But one of the most lamentable faults of the namedropper is his preference for the best-sounding names rather than the best-sounding musicians. Just as the classical namedropper is always best advised to drop Stockhausen rather than Bach, so his jazz counterpart is far wiser to talk about his acquaintance with Beiderbecke rather than his friendship with Bix, even though the two references apply to the same man. The counter-revolutionary jazz namedroppers of the 1940s could quite easily gather a large crowd of adoring neophytes simply by discussing the relative merits of Teschmaker and Stuhlmaker, neither of which players ever contributed a tenth as much to the jazz art as Fats or Fatha or Little Benny. Fortunately this practice died out from the moment that the long-playing era swept away the trainspotters of jazz whose tastes were influenced less by the merits of the music than by the obscurity of the musician and the unavailability of his recordings.

Because today Jazz is the common man's cultural bandwagon, the number of practised namedroppers has become too vast for the comfort of the insiders, who have tried to protect the rarity of their status by altering the namedropping

rules as they go. Thus an ambitious but inexpert namedropper might refer to Basie, learn the error of his ways and
get used to talking about The Count, add the final polish
by reducing the name to Count, only to learn to his understandable bewilderment that inside the sanctum sanctorum of
Jazz Basie is always known as Bill. For those who prefer to
drop their names on paper, or critics, as they are often referred to, there are certain knotty textual points to be considered. Anyone who writes 'Bix' insted of Bix is instantly
revealed as a Philistine or philly, and as for the man who
commits to paper a solecism like J. J. Johnson for
Jay Jay Johnson, he will be beyond the hipster's pale for
all time.

When in company the jazz namedropper has to be very
careful to match the names he is dropping with the right
accompaniment. It is tragic to say 'Brubeck swings, my friend',
better to amend it to 'Dave swings, man,' best of all to remark 'Dave swings, baby.' The fact that Dave has never
succeeded in swinging in his life has nothing to do with it.
Namedropping and artistic ability have not the remotest
connection. As for the creeping advance of the word 'baby',
this is the phenomenon of the 1960s and has quickly become
a vital trick in the game. It is probably harmless, and only
becomes really confusing when the subject under discussion
happens to be the technique of the New Orleans veteran
drummer Warren 'Baby' Dodds. In this situation remarks
are apt to fly like 'Baby plays like a baby, baby,' at which
point the second party, always assuming he is conversant
with the rules of the game, will hedge by plunging into a
discussion of the relative plunger-mute techniques of Bubber
and Cootie, or the degree to which the repeal of Prohibition
affected the styles of Muggsy and Wingy, or which of the
three legendary Johnsons, Bunk, Keg or Dink, was the biggest
fraud.

This dramatic rise of the Baby Syndrome in jazz has of
course played havoc with the position of women, who, so
far as jazz is concerned, are among the greatest namedroppers
in the business. There is a great deal more petticoat government in the jazz world than the outsider realises, and when
one of the matriarchs hears her man repeatedly addressing
other men as 'baby', there is a distinct danger of the entire
social fabric falling apart. At the moment, however, the
women are just about holding their own, and, being like all
other women, continue to show an instinctive grasp of what

will and what will not enhance their sex appeal. Jazz's female namedroppers realised many years and hundreds of styles ago that the Bubber-Tick-Zinkie ploy was essentially unfeminine, and soon evolved their own style of namedropping which might fairly be called the Bourgeois Reaction.

On the lips of women all jazz names worth the dropping take on an innocence so pristine as to be hardly recognisable. Cannonball Adderley becomes Julian, Lockjaw Davis turns magically into an innocuous Edward, while Peewee Russell undergoes a complete change of personality by being referred to as Charles Ellsworth. Probably this is a subconscious attempt by women to bowdlerise the men in the jazz world and, if so, there is a great deal of logic in the strategy. Presumably it is much easier to control a man called Ferdinand than it is to live with one called Jelly Roll, especially if the neighbours are aware of the connotations of the nickname.

In Britain the art of dropping illustrious jazz names is sadly limited for obvious reasons, Jazz being the one art form where not one name worth the dropping has been produced by this country. In such a world, so insular and so ill-informed, it is actually possible to experience the ultimate at the hands of a namedropper, which is to have one's own name dropped in casual conversation. A few years ago a man I had never seen before and have never seen since, remarked to me, 'I dig Benny Green's work, don't you?' My confusion was compounded by the fact, which my acquaintance may or may not have known, that there is in America another musician called Bennie Green whose skill as a trombonist really makes our name worth dropping.

The most awkward predicament of all, however, is created, not by the truly gifted namedropper, but by the aspiring apprentice fired by all the necessary enthusiasm and lacking totally in the required finesse. One evening towards the end of my playing days, at just about the time that 'baby' was taking over from 'man', I became involved in a jazz club conversation with a cluster of instrumentalist friends all well versed in the latest amendments to the hipster's vocabulary. The conversation became a discussion, the discussion a debate, and the debate, inevitably, a fierce argument. Our voices rose. Several paying customers stood listening to the row, whose central issue I can no longer remember. Gradually the dispute resolved itself, the vocabulary reverted back to the bourgeois norm and our group dispersed. As I stood there, one of the eavesdroppers approached holding an autograph book. It was a young girl of that truly delightful shape and poundage the jazz environment has always excelled in producing.

'Excuse me,' she said, 'but would you please put your name in my book, Mr Baby?'

As I wrote 'Mr Baby' in her book, I remember wondering what Duke or T-Bone or Lady or Prez or Crackpot or Stove-pipe or Blind Lemon or Bogus Ben would have done. Nothing, probably.

THE CULTURE CULTS

In the early 1940s two events occurred which galvanised the world of jazz, until then a sleepy backwater with almost no critical history at all. Somebody discovered that William 'Bunk' Johnson was still alive, at least in the biological sense, and an unknown saxophonist called Charlie Parker realised that chromatic harmony was by no means beyond the scope of the jazz instrumentalist. It was these two discoveries that created for the first time the ideal conditions for fashion and cultism to thrive. Until now, there had simply been jazz. Either you liked it or you didn't, although there had been some critical sniping before this, particularly among those who, for reasons best known to themselves, felt obliged to choose between the two great trumpeters of the 1920s. Bix Beiderbecke and Louis Armstrong. Beiderbecke, being white and dead, held all the aces here, but the only real point at issue was who should be placed first or second in the Great-ness Stakes. What followed in the wake of Johnson and Parker was something quite different. The tiny principality of jazz suddenly found itself split clean down the middle. Johnson was a sexagenarian New Orleans trumpeter unheard of for at least twenty years, and the archeologists who dug him up in-sisted on a new criterion of judging jazzmen which may briefly be summarised as the Age Before Beauty theory. Indeed, the fact that by 1940 Johnson was playing third-rate jazz strictly from memory only seemed to add spice to the wooing that fol-lowed. Parker, on the other hand, began to introduce into the jazz context sounds which appeared blasphemous to the New Orleans revivalists, bewildering to critics with no technical armoury and baffling to the layman, still fondly clinging to his dream of jazz as a goodtime music synonymous with bootlegging, chorus girls and sexual high jinks. From now on everyone hastily arraigned himself on one side or the other, armed himself with a few dirty adjectives, and started the Ancient versus Modern War, or Trad versus Bebop, as it came to be known inside the business.

Each camp was well stocked with crackpots determined to impose their own definitions of jazz on all the other crack-pots. Some young men tried to reproduce in the flesh the sound which Johnson had produced in the recording studio, reminiscent of a bunch of street musicians playing in the middle of a sandstorm. Other young men tried to copy the Parker mannerisms with the same relentless lack of logic, and one over-zealous British modernist actually went to Charing Cross Hospital in search of an injection which would make him coloured and thus bring him closer to Parker's muse.

But there was still one ingredient missing from the recipe, money. Jazz finances up till now were still small beer, but as the two factions, still locked in deadly combat rolled dusty and bruised into the 1950s, the advent of the long-playing record and a sudden gushing of jazz criticism whipped up so great an interest that profits started to rise and the outside world of culture began to sit up and take notice. Jazz suddenly became invested with overwhelming significance, artistic, psychological, sociological, political. Sometimes even music was brought into the argument, although not very often.

The Beboppers, now dignified by the term Modernists, began to win the war hands down. Johnson slid back into the miasma of jazz legend, his imitators graduated to the music-hall stage, where their gaily coloured waistcoats and tuppence-coloured advertising methods assured them a rich bonanza, while the Modernists were left more or less in possession of the field. Now the press agents and advertising managers began to move in. Before very long, a pianist called Dave Brubeck was on the front cover of *Time,* and another pianist, John Lewis, was buying his suits in Savile Row.

Brubeck and Lewis are vitally important in any study of jazz cultism because they were the first men to acquire the aura of a Brand Image. But apart from the fact that both of them realised the desirability of being the inspiration for a myth, their approaches were antipathetic. Lewis is the pro-totype of the modern egghead jazzman. University studies in Anthropology had led him to the curious conclusion that what jazz needed was Dignity. He was repelled by the old New Orleans bordello tradition, and longed to give the music Respectability, which he did by dubbing his compositions with French titles, dressing his quartet like undertakers and by eliminating the Smile from all public occasions. A typical MJQ album cover of the early days usually showed four men in morning coats looking at the camera with the studied gloom of four Eminent Victorians who have just heard about 'The Origin of Species'.

All this was enough to make people stop and look. Lewis's next problem was how to make them listen. This he achieved by respecting one of the oldest rules of human intercourse, which is that people will strain to listen to any old platitude, so long as you utter it quietly enough. Lewis's Modern Jazz Quartet made so little noise that a spectator sitting at the back of a large concert hall might have been forgiven for assuming that it was Lewis who pioneered current miming techniques.

If Lewis's policy was Conquest by Persuasion, Brubeck's was Conquest by Flattery. Brubeck began by flattering himself and then finished the job by extending his approval to the audiences. First he would announce his next piece and underline the difficulties about to be encountered by himself and his musicians, rather like the illusionist who tells his audience his next trick is impossible. Then he would arrive at the ultimate flattery by telling his customers what the trick was called. This was most devious, because with a title like 'Blues Rondo à la Turk,' the implication was that you and I were readily familiar, not only with blues, but also with rondos and with Turks. This appeal to the culture-vulture proved irresistible and, while Brubeck conducted his triumphal processional around the world, his fans began using Brubeck LP covers as complimentary tickets for entry into the world's cultural pantheon. It was easier than reading *War and Peace* or listening to Brahms symphonies, and it had the extra advantage of being unassailably, indisputably modern.

Since Lewis and Brubeck, nobody has enjoyed quite so loftily an eminence, although the saxophonist Gerry Mulligan has appeared in whisky ads. Recently *Time* extended its accolade to that professional eccentric among jazzmen, Thelonious Monk, of whose piano playing it has been re-marked, 'On the surface it's deep, but deep down it's shallow,' but it is doubtful whether any future stars will ever recapture the first fine careless rapture of John Lewis's goatee or Brubeck's genial giglamps.

A percentage of jazz fans continue to be guided in the record shops by the pictures on the album covers rather than the music between those covers. There has been a distinct advance in taste here. In the 1950s a Chet Baker album was adorned with a photo of a young lady stripped to the waist, clutching a teddy bear against each breast, precisely the kind of thing that Lewis has always fought against. Today the same album would probably be decorated by a Turner landscape or a Klee abstract. The music, however, would remain the same, a point of little interest to some customers.

For all the journalistic frenzy and the mass hero-worship, true reputations in jazz have fluctuated very little. Duke Ellington, who led the best big band of the late 1920s, still leads the best big band. Charlie Parker who died in 1925 still represents the furthest advance so far by the individual jazz musician. And the record companies remain neither less nor more knowledgeable about the products they are peddling than they were thirty years ago. In the monthly puff issued by one of our major companies there recently appeared the judgement that the two most accomplished string bassists in jazz were Charles Mingus and Oscar Peterson. Oscar Peterson plays the piano.

Complimentary Copy

GOODMAN 1963

When Mr Khrushchev remarked of the Benny Goodman Orchestra's tour of Russia last year, 'It's not jazz, only dance music,' he may not have said anything very profound, but he was certainly qualifying for the title of Head of State Most Likely to Succeed, at least so far as the jazz world is concerned.

If 'Benny Goodman in Moscow' is anything to judge by, Goodman did indeed play a great deal of dance music. Where Mr Khrushchev and many others seem to have confused the issue is in failing to realise that dance music is exactly what jazz is supposed to be. What Mr Khrushchev was probably trying to say was that Goodman had played the wrong kind of dance music, and he may well be right.

However, be it on Mr Khrushchev's head. The reasons for selecting Goodman, and not say, Duke Ellington or Louis Armstrong, for the first jazz tour of the Soviet Union, are enough to make a cat laugh. The Russians felt that Goodman was suitable because he played 'organised music' by which they evidently meant that he had an orchestra which reads from manuscript. There was also the point in his favour that Goodman had been known to play classical music, although the ability to play the Mozart Clarinet Concerto, or even the Artie Shaw Clarinet Concerto, is hardly a recommendation in the jazz world. Richest of all was the Soviets' consideration that Goodman's family 'came from Russia.' They did indeed, probably with a few dozen Cossacks chasing after them. . . .

Perhaps what rattled Mr Khrushchev was Goodman's insistence on playing the same type of orchestration, more or less, which made him the collegiate idol of the Roosevelt era. The sight of a once-honoured soloist being left high and dry by the tides of fashion is not an uncommon one in the jazz world, with its hysterical rate of evolution. Nobody expects an old dog to learn new tricks, certainly, but Goodman's trouble seems to be that he has forgotten how to perform the old ones.

The moment of truth comes in the quintet medley, the small group formula Goodman used nearly thirty years ago to achieve a marvellous synthesis of clarinet style. In the Moscow recordings, the technique remains intact, but the sense of form, that gift for weaving a succession of phrases into a single entity, once Goodman's most effective weapon, seems to have dissolved on the winds of middle age.

Goodman plays 'Avalon', 'World is Waiting for the Sunrise', 'Rose Room', all the themes with a long Goodman history, and not once does the old spark appear, except from pianist Teddy Wilson, whose talent would seem to be more durable than Goodman's. To compare the leader's playing with that of two of the hired hands, Zoot Sims and Phil Woods, would be too callous, but to his credit Goodman did recruit a talented unit, and whipped it into shape with great efficiency.

The burden of the past is inescapable for Goodman, but it is hard to understand the actions of others of his generation who deliberately bring trouble on their own heads. *Count Basie and the Kansas City Seven* is a reasonable enough production, but its title must have been chosen by a masochist. The original Kansas City Seven, recruited by Basie in 1936, produced some of the greatest jazz recordings of all time. The new recording, by borrowing an old title, is asking for comparison, gets comparison, and quietly curls up and dies.

Stan Getz, having committed that gross breach of tact, a hit record, may well complain that the rest of his output is being overlooked in the process. *Jazz Samba*, the album which accidentally started a bossa nova craze, contains the original 'Desafinado', but it also includes several other plums. Getz's highly stylised perfection on 'Samba Dese Days' and 'Baia' is remarkable to listen to. This is surely one of the finest albums by a saxophonist in a long time.

GOODMAN 1964

Certain occasions stand out in jazz history so vividly that after a time sentiment begins to rear its beguiling head. The 1789 of jazz may be said to be the successful assault of the

Benny Goodman Orchestra on Carnegie Hall on the night of January 16, 1938. It was the largest single step which jazz had taken up to that time in its curious and comical quest for social respectability, and was the precursor of the contemporary trend for endless festivals and concert tours.

The history of the recording of that singular night's work is a little difficult to comprehend, for after the belated release in this country of *Goodman at Carnegie Hall*, the two-volume album was deleted after a comparatively short period, presumably because nobody was buying. This month the same company has reissued the same albums with new covers. From the point of view of the technical addicts, the new issue is far better than the old, for the engineers have done an excellent cleaning job on the record surfaces, and there must be many people who delayed buying the first issue until it was too late.

Although Goodman's achievement in filling Carnegie Hall with a jazz show has tremendous symbolic significance, it has to be admitted that at least half of the music is distinctly unmemorable, and that most of the rest of it is merely a duplication of the many studio recordings of Goodman during the same period. However, it is hard to overrate Jess Stacy's rollicking piano solo on 'One O'Clock Jump' and the many examples of Goodman's scholastic clarinet playing, which had by this time arrived at the point of perfect balance between the gusto of the Chicagoans and the academic severity brought about by classical studies. But after all this time it is more apparent than ever that the Goodman small group apart, the best music that night at Carnegie Hall was provided by the guests from the great coloured orchestras of the day. Johnny Hodges from the Ellington band, in an amazing, ravishing performance on 'Blue Prelude', and Lester Young, from the Basie band, producing in 'Honeysuckle Rose' aphoristic subtleties astonishing for the times.

No doubt a few of today's recordings will endure as long as the Goodman at Carnegie Hall album, but it is not always easy to believe it. One album which may be delighting the next generation is one with the unfortunate title of *Them Dirty Blues* featuring the Cannonball Adderley Quintet. The leader's alto saxophone playing strikes a powerful blow for the modern cause, because it proves beyond any reasonable doubt that jazz is not dying of a surfeit of harmony.

Cannonball employs the device of heavily accented quavers to push the beat along, and has the advantage of a faultless

89

rhythm section. On tracks like 'Work Song' and 'Dat Dere' he produces solos as finely integrated and as imaginative as anything recorded since the death of Charlie Parker, on whom he leans stylistically rather less heavily than Sonny Stitt.

Stitt's new album, *Sonny Stitt Blows the Blues*, demonstrates again Stitt's impressive consistency. He is one of jazz's most prolific recorders, and rarely uses any devices to create any orchestral contrast. Once again he simply stands before a rhythm section and improvises, most of the time employing the classic twelve-bar blues form.

Far less ingenious than Stitt but perhaps more bewitching is the veteran tenor saxophonist Ben Webster, who in *Ben Webster Meets Oscar Peterson* suggests he is completely unaware of the passing of time and that the conventional picture of a saxophone player is of a frenzied young man. Webster is one of those players, like Paul Gonsalves and Johnny Hodges, whose tone is so beautiful that he would still be an attractive player even if he produced strings of solecisms.

But Webster is one of the most cunning of improvisers. Although he appears on the surface to be merely embroidering the melody rather than improvising upon it, several careful hearings of his work reveal that he is able to imbue any old theme with a fresh lease of life. On his liaison with Peterson there is one remarkable demonstration of this. The four-man group play 'Bye Bye Blackbird', begin quite mildly, slowly build to an unforced climax and then gracefully fall away to the dying cadences of the performance. It is a superb example of the miraculous vitality of jazz at its best.

GOODMAN 1969

As Virginia Woolf almost put it, human nature changed on New Year's Eve 1942, at least so far as the jazz world was concerned. On that day the Big Band era, that spectacular and wholly accidental chapter in musical public relations drew to a close and its supporters drifted on to the next sideshow. At the Paramount Theatre in New York, Frank Sinatra, himself a product of the big band, opened his solo career and marked the exact point at which the singers took over.

For the musicians it had been a brief but brilliant innings, which had begun when clarinettist Benny Goodman discovered by mistake that there existed a vast potential audience for jazz-tinged dance music. It was to prove the last time the general public was ever able to keep in step with jazz, and by a priceless irony it was the Goodman Orchestra which shared the bill with Sinatra that day at the Paramount.

The irony is compounded this month by the simultaneous appearance of three-volumed sets of both Goodman and Sinatra, and because he is very much more a relic of the past, it is to Goodman that the attention is diverted. Four years almost to the day after that Sinatra concert, Goodman disbanded his group and beguiled his semi-retirement with the pleasures of what used to be known as classical music. But every so often he felt the old urge, and may fairly be said to have made more farewell appearances than all the prima donnas of the nineteenth century put together. *Benny Goodman Swing Classics* is the result of one of these returns, in the mid 1950s.

His band, which appeared for a few weeks in a New York night club, was a most uncharacteristic compromise between the small group and full orchestral formulas Goodman had favoured in the past. He was now leading an octet, and the probability that he did not quite know what to do with it is suggested by the fact that for most of the three albums it is the four central members of the band, the rhythm section and Goodman himself, who take the lion's share of the playing.

The standard of musicianship on all twenty-nine tracks is extremely high, and the doubts about its quality which caused the long delay in a British release are dispelled by the playing of Urbie Green (trombone) and Ruby Braff (cornet), the style of Teddy Wilson's piano playing and, of course, the blatant technical mastery of Goodman himself. Watching the cracks gradually appear in the smooth façade of Goodman's style is one of the most intriguing of all jazz studies. It is usually conceded that by the start of the 1960s a few of those cracks had become embarrassingly wide, but at the time he made these albums Goodman was still a brilliant jazz clarinettist who, in spite of his age and vast experience, was still able occasionally to become involved.

By an odd chance the best track is also the one in which the telltale signs appear most clearly. In 'I Found a New Baby' Goodman suddenly manages to turn himself on and races away for several choruses, all of which demonstrate his unique contribution to the jazz art, that theoretically impossible blend of the conservatory and the speakeasy. And yet each time he arrives at the sixteenth bar of the song, the point where he must move into his middle section, Goodman betrays a hint of indecision, as though having been faced with this problem several million times before, he is at last weary of thinking up fresh variations. For this reason, that they show Goodman approaching the last crisis of his jazz career, these albums are poignant as well as musically rewarding.

By contrast, the reissue of the Sinatra set *His Greatest Years* is an anti-climax. As he showed in London last Monday, Sinatra still has a long way to go before being handed over to history, so that these thirty-six tracks, covering the years 1953–60, hardly have the extra appeal of pastness.

But several of the performances are vocal classics, 'When Your Lover Has Gone' and 'Put Your Dreams Away' are two of the best ballad recordings Sinatra has achieved, and 'One For My Baby' with its honky-tonk piano backing and its inspired reading of Johnny Mercer's wry lyric, is probably the best musical telling of a short story in the repertoire of popular music.

HENDERSON 1964

Nobody contributed more to the evolution of the large jazz band than Fletcher Henderson, an indifferent pianist, a poor disciplinarian and an absymal exploiter of his own wares, but a man with much instinctive wisdom in his musical approach. *The Fletcher Henderson Story – a Study in Frustration* is a magnificent production showing that Henderson always subordinated his orchestral ambitions to the ability of his soloists, instead of reversing the procedure – like so many of the leaders who usurped his position in the palmy days of the 1930s.

Henderson led a large orchestra from 1923 to 1934 and the value of this four-volume issue lies in the fact that his progress can be charted almost from month to month.

At first the orchestral methods were crude and clumsy. In volumes one and two are to be found all the indulgence of the period, particularly the simulation of train and animal noises, and that curious obsession of jazz in the 1920s with the depiction of bogus orientalism, resulting in oddities like 'Shanghai Shuffle'. At this stage the orchestra is merely an impediment to the enjoyment of superlative instrumental playing by Louis Armstrong and Coleman Hawkins.

Armstrong in 'How Come You Do Me Like You Do' plays with marvellous restrained power and wit, but he hardly eclipses the lesser-known Joe Smith, who, in 'What Cha Call 'Em Blues', playing a trumpet solo which is all charm and modesty, supports the theory of many musicians that the cornetist Bix Beiderbecke modelled his style closely on Smith's.

By the late 1920s Henderson was learning how to blend scored passages into a succession of solos, and although by this time Armstrong had moved on, the individual talent in the ranks remained undimmed. Musicians like Fats Waller, Benny Carter, Rex Stewart, Jimmie Harrison, Buster Bailey and Tommy Ladnier were eager to work for Henderson, who gradually evolved many of the tricks of style fated to become clichés a few years later in the hands of Benny Goodman and the Dorsey Brothers.

The question-and-answer choruses of saxophone and trumpet sections that later brought into being a nation of jitterbugs, the crisply scored ensembles that were really jazz solos written down and multiplied to the power of three, the orchestral figures cunningly wrought so as to further excite the soloist, Henderson pioneered all these effects without ever winning any kind of financial reward.

Perhaps the saddest volume of the four is the last one, which sees Henderson attempting a comeback in 1936. If anything, the music is better than ever, but by now the white touring bands had relegated Henderson to comparative obscurity.

The solo playing on 'Stealin' Apples', performed by saxophonist Cha Berry and trumpeter Roy Eldridge, surely ranks among the finest jazz of the decade, surpassed orchestrally only by the Ellington and Basie bands of the period. That is why the volume's sub-title, 'A Study in Frustration', is especially apt.

The college-trained son of teaching parents, Henderson was too inhibited by the colour bar to pursue his ambitions to their logical end, and he must have accepted with mixed feelings the overwhelming commercial success of the Benny Goodman Orchestra, many of whose scores he wrote, and whose stylistic father he undoubtedly was. The sixty-four

93

tracks of his memorial album, fautlessly documented, are only a belated tribute to one of the most important pioneers in jazz history.

THE GOOD OLD DAYS 1965

Teachers in schools and institutes may soon find that a passing acquaintance with the laws of counterpoint and a smattering of musical history is inadequate for explaining jazz to children of all ages. *Jazz in the Making, the Classic Era* (Parlophone PMC 1195), is an anthology designed to resolve their dilemma.

The dilemma is a very real one, now that jazz is an official subject in the Adult Education department of the LCC. The compilers of 'Jazz in the Making' are therefore doing a most useful job. Their twelve selected tracks are musically valid, should have an immediate impact on ears sympathetic to but not intimately acquainted with jazz, and are, above all, representative of the period they attempt to cover. The anthology also carries an explanatory pamphlet which deals with first principles without being patronising.

The only musician to appear more than once in 'Jazz in the Making' is Louis Armstrong, but that was inevitable. He is heard twice with the Hot Five and once with a larger orchestra, and all three performances are superlative. But to show that Armstrong never appeared from out of a void, there is also a track by his early mentor King Oliver with Armstrong himself on second trumpet. To complicate the issue of influence and cross-influence still further, Henry Allen, an Armstrong disciple, appears in the last track on the album with the Luis Russell orchestra playing 'Panama'.

In a similar way the career of Bix Beiderbecke is sketched in through his two earliest inspirations, the Original Dixieland Jazz Band and the New Orleans Rhythm Kings. The Bix selection, *At the Jazz Band Ball* is hardly the best available, but to have preferred any of the more renowned Beiderbecke performances would have seemed like plumping for the obvious. The one track which will cause many sore heads in the common room is the original recording of Duke Ellington's 'Black and Tan Fantasy', which is primitive and yet profound, conventionally orchestral and yet utterly strange to the non-jazz ear. No amount of explanatory pamphleteering could explain this one away.

Teachers and pupils alike who manage to get through 'Jazz in the Making' without too much trouble may then care to tackle *Great Jazz Standards* on which the pianist Gil Evans orchestrates some of the best-known compositions from all eras. Evans has discovered that many early jazz themes written casually, with slapdash collective improvisation in mind, have distinct orchestral possibilities, and his settings of Beiderbecke's 'Davenport Blues' and Don Redman's 'Chant of the Weed' are ambitious enough to have astonished their composers, who never dreamed of such considerate treatment, although perhaps they deserved it.

For pupils who despair of ever reaching any kind of understanding, there appears this month a dazzling exposition of the master-pupil relationship in jazz. *Father of the Stride Piano* shows James P. Johnson in complete mastery of the resonant harmonic textures and intricate cross-rhythms of a style he virtually invented. In *The Amazing Fats Waller* one of Johnson's two most gifted pupils (the other was Duke Ellington), pays unconscious tribute to the wit and masculinity of Johnson's style with every bar he plays.

Not even Waller's lampoons of Scottish folk songs, and his preference on half the sixteen tracks for the organ instead of the piano, can hide the fact that his greatness as a jazz pianist stems from the days in the early 1920s when he and Duke Ellington would ply Johnson with drinks until the master would agree to give them a lecture from the piano keyboard.

EVEN OLDER DAYS 1965

There is no jazz musician so great as the one we have never actually heard. The early history of the music is peppered with these semi-mythical characters whose reputations flourish as their dates recede because little or no evidence exists to contradict those reputations.

Jazz Odyssey, Volume One, subtitled 'The Sound of New Orleans', will undoubtedly be pounced upon by the historians and the amateur musicologists, but it will also lay a few of those irritating ghosts who have been floating about for so long. The first instalment comes in three divisions; and is obviously the fruit of heroic labours by 'dedicated master-number detectives' in 'obscure warehouses and remote archives'. It is a romantic picture, but unfortunately remoteness and obscurity are not in themselves virtues, and the forty-eight performances are by no means all manifestations of genius.

The series begins at the beginning, literally, with the Original Dixieland Jazz Band in 'the first commercial recording for home gramophone reproduction of the sounds of a jazz band'. And appalling sounds they are, even for 1917. On the evidence of the ODJB's 'Darktown Strutter's Ball' it seems incredible that the cornet playing of their leader, Nick La Rocca, should have later inspired a teenaged Bix Beiderbecke to become a jazz musician.

The rest of the hallowed names come tumbling out: Fate Marable, Leon Rappolo, Bunk Johnson, Jim Robinson, Papa Celestin, and what emerges is the fact that public instinct over the years has been absolutely right. 'Jazz Odyssey' shows that Freddie Keppard was *not* a genius lost to posterity only because of his aversion to recording studios; that Leon Rappolo, even without his mental disintegration, would never have become the world's greatest clarinettist; that the Bunk Johnson revival was spurious because there was nothing to revive, and that all that was fine in the early music of New Orleans has been familiar to us for years.

All this is proved by the fact that some of 'Jazz Odyssey' is superlative stuff, form being the infallible guide. The outstanding musicians are those we might have expected to be outstanding. King Oliver obviously deserves much of his great posthumous reputation. Sidney Bechet's swaggering talent in 'Dear Old Southland' makes his rivals sound like pygmies, and Jimmie Noone's beautiful poise is very much more than a legend. Above all, in every sense of the term, there is Louis Armstrong, who appears with six different groups between 1923 and 1929, carrying them all on his shoulders, fully mature before the music itself was mature. No further proof is needed of Armstrong's almost godlike powers as a jazz musician, but, seen in the context of the 1920s, the whole thing begins to look unbelievable.

'Jazz Odyssey' is one of those rare productions whose historical interest overrides all musical faults. It is hard to see on what grounds it could be excluded from any comprehensive record collection. It has too many piquant moments for it to be ignored, and it does invaluable work in removing the artificial barriers of time and style which have sliced up the jazz lover's mind for so long. One track of 'Jazz Odyssey' actually has Artie Shaw playing in the same band as Jelly Roll Morton, and more than that nobody could possibly ask.

Morton was one of the great screwballs of modern times. Even by the standards of the world which raised him, the New Orleans of sixty years ago, the enormity of his pretension was a thing to gasp at. His modesty itself is streaked through with a comical egocentric magnanimity ('Please do not misunderstand me. I do not claim the creation of the Blues'), and his most famous pearl, 'Kansas City style, New Orleans style, Chicago style, they're all Jelly-Roll style', still has an Olympian ring about it. But the extravagance of his claims absolves us from the task of disproving them, and the appearance of *Jelly-Roll Morton, King of New Orleans Jazz,* gives us the chance to hear for ourselves what all the fuss was about.

It seems that Morton was one of those men who talk better than they play, for none of the music in this album possesses the fluency of his recorded autobiography, now in the Library of Congress in Washington. Certainly none of it contains the poetic flair with which Morton evoked the aura of his home town at the beginning of the new century. In his book *Mr Jelly Roll,* Alan Lomax strove heroically to make Morton's career all of a piece, even achieving the Freudian master-stroke of equating Morton's manner of trombone scoring with the search for a father-figure, and indeed he did succeed in establishing some excuse for the gap between Morton's claims and Morton's ability.

Morton's was a classic case of persecution mania. He was always convinced that life had conspired against him, and spent his later years grumbling about his neglect while lesser musicians thrived. And to Morton all other musicians were lesser musicians. It is true that he was one of the first to stumble on the paradox that a soloist might find an orchestrated background conducive to finer flights of improvised fancy. But a comparison of the newest revival album with the work of Duke Ellington at the same period, 1926–28, shows that Morton was hardly equipped to put into practice theories which were undoubtedly sound. The real failure of his orchestral attempts is proved by the fact that in this album the improvised passages are always more effective than the scored passages, ambitious though they may have been.

A few years before Morton recorded those sides, another son of New Orleans, Louis Armstrong, had made his first recordings with King Oliver's Creole Jazz Band, and in *Louis Armstrong, 1923,* we can appreciate the skilful way in which a great virtuoso, hired to play second cornet to the leader, subdued his brilliance for the sake of ensemble cohesion.

By the time Duke Ellington was writing for a twelve-piece orchestra, jazz had advanced far beyond the boundaries of Oliver and Morton. *Ellingtonia Volume Two*, recorded in the 1930s, already possesses orchestral textures Morton had never dreamed of, and original compositions displaying a melodic gift unmatched anywhere in jazz. 'I Let a Song Go Out of My Heart' and 'Solitiude' have defied the passing years and the passing fashions.

If the aggressively modern work of *Sonny Rollins and Clifford Brown* (Esquire EP 238) endures half as well, everyone will be surprised, for although Rollins and Brown display superb incandescent brilliance, they are perhaps too self-consciously determined to be children of their own times ever to be the children of any other.

JAZZ AND DRAMA *1961*

It is just possible that the music from *The Connection* will turn out to be the biggest-selling jazz album ever released in Britain, but only if the play settles in for a long run. The recording was made by the four men who introduced the music in the off-Broadway production, and only two of them, saxophonist Jackie McLean and pianist-composer Freddie Redd, appear in the anglicised version. But change of personnel is not the sole difference between the recording and the London production, which raises a most vital point.

Jazz being improvised music, and 'The Connection' having already played to live audiences for fifteen months before it came here, it must have been a temptation for Redd to amend the score and resort to any device which might preserve the eager aggression of the music. That is why the theatregoer who knows the Blue Note recording may be baffled. 'Who Killed Cock Robin' and 'O.D.' have both been replaced, and the blues which illustrates 'the humour and sadness of Sam's plea to the audience' appears in amended form. Redd has been shrewd enough to retain the best themes, and 'Music Forever', 'Time to Smile' and 'Sister Salvation' are outstanding. *Music Forever* is a curious motif. Intended as a paean symbolising the hipster's devotion to jazz, it is altogether too triumphant an affair which conjures up visions of quarter-backs galumphing over the gridiron rather than the slack-faced euphoria of the afterfix; but judged purely as a musical theme it is a neat example of Redd's talent for harmonic patterns which suggest melodic variations to the soloist.

On the one occasion when jazz is used as a background to the action rather than as the action itself, Redd employs a melody which balances itself beautifully between the mocking and the sentimental. 'Theme for Sister Salvation' is the only true programme music in the entire score, and the march figure played pianissimo by McLean is the one likely to stay in the mind the longest.

In the last reckoning, however, 'The Connection' recording will stand or fall purely on its musical merits; thus judged it falls just short of the highest contemporary standards. The interesting thing about it is that because of 'The Connection's' Chinese-box structure of play-within-a-film-within-a-play the music is dramatic without being theatrical, and therefore might have been the result of any night in a jazz club. That is why it is as good as it is.

MARTYRS AND JAZZMEN 1966
Four Lives in the Bepop Business, A. B. Spellman
Macgibbon & Kee 36s

As jazz is one of the two subjects on which everyone today professes to be an expert (the other is love), most books on the subject turn out to be long-winded exercises in the art of grinding the wrong axe. This is doubly true for the 1960s, when jazz, in a desperate attempt to pretend that the possibilities of improvising on a chord sequence are not finite, is contorting itself into postures so bizarre that even the very greatest jazzmen have trouble rationalising the findings of their fellow-workers. An entirely different and very funny book might be written explaining how it can be that music which baffles the practitioners can be so perfectly understood by men whose knowledge of music is more or less non-existent.

This is not to say that Spellman's book is hopeless. There are some good things to be found in it, not least a passionate indignation at the disgusting treatment meted out to the Negro artist in America. The text, outrageously padded as it is with transcripts of taped conversations, does give some idea of the confused battle for self-expression which the American

Negro is so desperately fighting. It is perfectly true that Spell-man's four eponymous heroes, saxophonists Ornette Cole-man and Jackie McLean, pianists Cecil Taylor and Herbie Nicols, are men who, by the very definition of their race and profession, are victims of a society too crass to realise that jazz has been North America's one original contribution to the art of the twentieth century. It is true also that jazz to-day is in dire need of innovation. And it is truest of all that unless people like Coleman and company are given their heads, the music may well shrivel up and die before very long.

Unfortunately, none of this has anything to do with the point Spellman is trying to make, which is that his four heroes are great musicians being deprived of their own genius by the machinery of persecution and intolerance. As none of the four selected martyrs are in fact geniuses at all, or at least have never produced any evidence to suggest they are, the author's thesis is suddenly seen to be sociological rather than musical, and for this reason irritating to anybody seek-ing enlightenment about music.

All four of Spellman's subjects are or were revolutionaries of a kind and for that reason a certain wild glamour attaches to them. But in order to assess the validity of any revolution it is just as well if one knows something about the status quo, and it is here that Spellman's book finally puts itself hope-lessly out of court. Not once in the 241 pages is there the slightest indication that the author understands, or is even very interested in, the basic principles of musical form, grammar or syntax. The resulting effect is rather like that of a blind man trying to enjoy a visit to the Tate on the entirely honourable assumption that modern art is good for the people.

But *Four Lives* is an intensely interesting book, even if for the wrong reasons. Without question it is the prototype for many more to come, in which aesthetic considerations will be so hopelessly confused with the socio-political ones that the poor reader will no longer know whether he is sup-posed to be tapping his foot or sharpening his sword. As a historian and poet, Spellman should have known better than to assume that art propagated in a worthy cause is necessarily worthy art.

JAZZ IN THE BEGINNING 1968
Early Jazz, by Gunther Schuller
(Oxford, 55s)

I think it was Neville Cardus who once derided that school of criticism which tries to evaluate a composer by counting the notes in his works. And I seem to remember Corno di Bassetto having something appropriately offensive to say about the ridiculous parsing which passed for musical criticism in the nineteenth century. It would now seem that the disease has spread to jazz. It had to come, of course, if only as a reaction against the tide of inane jive-talk and sloppy reminiscence the jazz world has been disgorging for so long, but there is a dangerous temptation to swing too far the other way and reduce jazz to an arid intellectual exercise.

Schuller, an American composer who for some years has trodden ponderous measures on the fringe of jazz, is one of those well-intentioned textual analysts who evidently believe that the beauty of St Paul's can be explained away by describing the composition of the bricks. The first volume of his jazz history is the perfect example of the man whose ear is so close to the ground that he cannot see the landscape.

Schuller's avowed purpose is to scrap the legends and get on with the music. He seems quite unaware that legends always contain a grain of truth and that the way to proceed is not to ignore them but to rationalise them. Thus he can write of Bix Beiderbecke, 'From this area of conflict and others he turned to escape such as liquor.' Apart from the execrable prose, the statement is terrifyingly imperceptive as an explanation for Beiderbecke's artistic fecklessness and the pathetic gulf between his training and his sensibilities. Much worse is Schuller's fundamental error in ascribing to a wholly intuitive artist like Louis Armstrong all kinds of harmonic stratagems. Like his French counterpart André Hodeir, Schuller works out the velocity of the flying oranges and then compliments the juggler on being a Senior Wrangler.

The one area where this kind of method can be of real value is orchestral jazz where strategy and forethought do exist and are indeed of vital importance. The chapter on Duke Ellington's early years is finely researched and acutely observed, as we all acknowledged eight years ago when it first appeared in a jazz anthology. Schuller is a patently well-meaning man who loves the music very much. But like Hodeir, he sounds totally devoid of any sense of humour. It may or may not be significant that both men have at different times tried their hands at playing jazz, and that the musical result was as cold and impersonal as their criticism. It is a good, and for jazz a very necessary, thing to distinguish texts from the legends that surround them, but Schuller, too solemn for his own good, has thrown out the baby with the bath water.

NOISES FROM THE ALLEY* 1965

The one vital truth about Tin Pan Alley is the fact that for all the sentimentality of its inmates so dutifully taking in each other's washing, it is an industry catering for children. Its output is the musical equivalent of 'Comic Cuts', except that the editors of penny comics never dreamed of claiming for their wares the slightest aesthetic significance.

As the spectacle of grown men pandering to the uninformed tastes of juveniles is fundamentally a ridiculous one, the most effective method of composing a confessional from inside the castle is straightfaced understatement. Mr Rogers seems to have grasped the first half of this proposition but not the second. Realising the hopelessness of explaining away the great mound of garbage sedulously compiled by Tin Pan Alley since the war, he opts insteads for candour, but is unable to repress the self-pride bubbling in his breast. The result is a disastrous amalgam of jocoseness and schoolboy naughtiness which soon becomes maddening.

Somewhere in the course of his rambling, slightly hysterical story, Mr Rogers revives the old chestnut about the songwriter ejected from a publisher's office because his music is too good. As he tumbles downstairs, the songwriter, who is carrying an accordion, falls on the instrument and produces a ghastly discord, at which the publisher rushes out, dusts him down, and says, 'Why on earth didn't you play that one first?' The story is too old to be funny, but it is symptomatic of the double-think which ails Tin Pan Alley, an awareness of its own worthlessness coupled with the belief that to acknowledge this worthlessness and still persist, somehow makes all the inmates heroic and even rather lovable.

* *Tin Pan Alley,* by Eddie Rogers as told to Mike Hennessey (Hale, 18s).

The most telltale anecdote of all concerns a photograph of twenty-seven of Britain's most successful bandleaders. Apparently all twenty-seven turned up without payment as a gesture of friendship towards the author, who was so moved that he began to cry. The photograph has already passed into the folklore of Tin Pan Alley, but what is most revealing is the fact that at no point does Mr Rogers stop to think what this ridiculous crew of bow-tied popinjays might actually sound like. Which is perfectly logical. If ever it stopped to think what the music sounded like, Tin Pan Alley would be lost.

Broadway

In 1967 a *Punch* essayist, extracting what humour he could from the jazz life, in passing lamented the fact that I appeared to be becoming progressively more distracted from my jazz interests by musical comedy, much as to say that it is a sad portent for the future of theology when the monks start frequenting the local brothel. I was not sure of the exact point of the observation, but understood it to mean that the demands of jazz criticism are too rigorous for any man to be able to meet them for very long without risking permanent damage to his mental faculties. Although I thought I recognised a grain of truth in the idea, I considered its generalisations to be too sweeping, but, rather flattered that anyone should have bothered to observe my movements at all, kept my objections to myself. In any case, I had by then already been writing about jazz in continuing good health, for long enough for the mere fact of my survival to be in itself a sufficient contradiction of the theory. I have to admit, however, that a great many people believe that Jazz and Musical Comedy are incompatible, and frankly I find this extraordinary.

For it so happens that the world of jazz and the musical stage, so far from being antipathetic, are aesthetically much more closely allied than the friendly reproach in *Punch* would imply. In fact, the proposition that there are moments when the two have become so intertwined as to have become very nearly the same thing might be an extremely difficult one to discredit. Consider, for instance, my own experiences as an apprentice musician. The first recordings which influenced my conception of how jazz ought to be played were the Billie Holiday-Teddy Wilson pickup bands and the assorted small groups formed by Benny Goodman, both of which series of recordings I started acquiring through the 1940s with as much speed as a teenage budget and the delays of wartime would allow. By 1945 I had gathered enough items to start making a few deductions, one of which was that without Broadway, it might have been difficult at times for the jazz musician to know what to play. Among my Goodman items were 'Lady Be Good', 'I Know That You Know', 'I Surrender Dear', 'Exactly Like You', 'More Than You Know', 'Body and Soul', 'I Got Rhythm'. Billie Holiday had recorded 'Summertime', 'I've Got My Love To Keep Me Warm', 'More Than You Know', 'Can't Help Loving That Man', 'The Man I Love', 'Night and Day', 'Why Was I Born?' and 'I Can't Get Started'. I also possessed the famous Lester Young recordings of 'Lady Be Good' and 'Lester Leaps In' (a disguised version of 'I Got Rhythm'), also Hawkins' 'Out of Nowhere' and 'Body and Soul'. For a time I was too preoccupied by the astonishing inventiveness displayed on these recordings to start theorising about their genesis. But the day had to come when I began drawing conclusions.

I have listed nineteen items, four of which occur twice, leaving fifteen actual compositions. Fourteen of them come from either musical comedy or revue, and the only way in which the fifteenth item, 'I've Got My Love to Keep Me Warm', differs from the others is that it was written for Hollywood instead of Broadway, which, so far as musical comedy is concerned, is no difference at all, as all the outstanding Broadway composers were eventually enticed out to Hollywood. Soon I started to break down the fifteen items in a different way, discovering that the name Gershwin appeared four times, Johnny Green, Vincent Youmans and Jerome Kern twice each, Irving Berlin, Vernon Duke and Cole Porter once each. Of course I possessed other recordings, and of course the names of other composers were often mentioned, but I list these names because of the consistency with which they began to confront me. Nor did their dominance fade when jazz styles altered. Indeed Modernism, when it arrived, paid Broadway the ultimate tribute of burglarising it so persistently that before long there was nobody apart from the musicians themselves who could be sure what was and what was not being played. 'Rifftide' was really 'Lady Be Good', 'Hot House' was 'What is This Thing Called Love?', 'Bird Gets the Worm' was 'Lover Come Back to Me', 'Anthropology' was 'I Got Rhythm', 'Ornithology' was 'How High the Moon', 'Koko' was 'Cherokee' and so on. And where the camouflage was dispensed with, the preponderance of Broadway became more noticeable than ever. The greatest soloist of the movement was Charlie Parker, and his recordings of the period which I possessed included 'Why Do I Love You?', 'All the Things You Are', 'Smoke Gets In Your Eyes' and 'The Song Is You', all by Kern, 'Embraceable You' and 'Strike Up the Band', both by Gershwin, Johnny Green's three outstanding songs, 'Body and Soul', 'Out of Nowhere' and 'I Cover the Waterfront', one item from Rodgers and Hart, 'I Didn't Know What Time It Was' and two by Vernon Duke, 'I Can't Get Started' and 'Autumn in New York'.

Even in the midst of the excitement of the discovery of these performances, by Billie Holiday and Benny Goodman, Charlie Parker and Dizzy Gillespie, even in the grip of my midsummer madness, a kind of notated frenzy which did not in fact subside for twenty years and from which I have never completely recovered, there was a kind of half-realisation somewhere at the back of my mind that the source of this music must surely be located at a considerable distance from the jazz world. There were occasional brief overtones in the performances, especially the vocal recordings, which could only be explained with reference to some other system of thought, some other world whose motives and actions were very different from those of Billie Holiday or Coleman Hawkins.

It needs to be said that during all the time I was acquainting myself with this body of recorded jazz, I never once saw a musical comedy, and it was not until 1954 and the London revival of 'Pal Joey' that I witnessed for the first time the creaking artifice and unique logic of the musical. However, long before I ever set eyes on 'Pal Joey', that curious mutilation by an author of his own original work, I had already weathered the storms in a thousand teacups of Fred Astaire and Ginger Rogers, Nelson Eddy and Jeanette MacDonald, Judy Garland and Mickey Rooney, Alice Faye and John Payne, Crosby, Oakie, Durbin and all the rest of the two-dimensional warblers whose careers happened, most unfortunately, to coincide with the perfection of a machine which took audiences down gullets magnified ten thousandfold by the miracles of modern technology. My long if quite accidental education in the art of the musical taught me among other things that those enchanting verses, on whose construction composers and lyricists often seemed to lavish more attention than they did on the choruses, and which to this day are usually neglected by professional singers, were not the gratuitous artistic flourishes I once thought they were, but had been originally designed for the strictly functional purpose of making bridges to span that awkward gap in conception between dialogue and song. And as my jazz education proceeded it became clear to me that, by some vast irony, none of the artists for whom these songs had originally been commissioned had ever been able to extract from them anything like the same depths of passion as the jazz champions, which means, among other things, that to this day, having once been infected by the art of Billie Holiday, I can never take the great mistresses of the musical comedy world seriously. I am sometimes told that in comparing a Billie Holiday with, say, an Ethel Merman or a Judy Garland I am confusing two categories. But a song is a song, and I am confusing nothing. I sometimes wonder if George Gershwin ever knew that the one occasion on which 'I Love You Porgy' was expressed with the dramatic intensity and earthy power it demands, was when Billie Holiday recorded it.

My faltering musical advance to professional status incorporated hundreds of nights on palais bandstands where the sheer wretchedness of most of the repertoire we were so handsomely paid to play forced me into other diversions, one of which was reading all the small print on my music parts, a diversion which not only acquainted me with the addresses and telephone numbers of every tripe-peddling music publisher in Britain, but also impressed on me yet again that whenever a song did happen to possess some kind of style, very likely it had been composed by one of that small group of composers, perhaps two dozen men who, I was now beginning to realise, represented a kind of professional elite. I noticed also that the number of new songs of this type appeared to be shrinking steadily, and that if the output of the Gershwins and the Kerns was anything to go by, there had been something very like a golden age between the two great wars, a period when apparently some sort of accidental balance had been struck between the sophistication of the best composers and the musical instincts of their audiences, before the moguls, mistaking their own musical imbecility for that of the general public, which really had quite good taste, had destroyed that balance by deliberately debasing the coinage of popular song.

Still later, I became a member of a co-operative group which, having no leader, was composed entirely of leaders, a unique fact of its existence which had a great deal to do with the impeccable government of its affairs and the immense success of its artistic policy. In this group, one of my extra-musical chores was to collect each night from the manager of whichever ballroom to which our agent had banished us, one of those printed sheets on which the performer is required to enter the titles and, where known, the authors of every song in his recital. The completed form is then sent to the Performing Right Society, which is thus able to gauge the frequency with which any song is being performed, and, therefore, the amount of the royalty accruing to each composer and lyricist. Now the co-operative group to which I refer was existing in the real world and not, sadly, in the Euphonia of Berlioz's dreams, which meant that we were obliged to include in our programmes at least a few items beneath our contempt. Under the circumstances the least I could do, on behalf of my partners as well as for myself, was to deprive the wretched composers of these wretched songs of the royalties to which they were rightfully entitled, by omitting their names from the sheet, which was filled instead with the names of my elite. My defence against accusations of unethical conduct is that I was at least meting out some kind of aesthetic justice, and that in any case, if the law will insist on equating three minutes of garbage with three minutes of artistry, then it must first breed a race of ballroom managers whose musical imbecility is mitigated by the ability to read the titles of songs on a slip of paper. Whether anyone ever analysed the sheets we returned each night I have no way of knowing, but on paper at least, we must have been the first jazz band in all history whose repertoire was limited to Gershwin and company.

It was around this period that, for a short interlude, a band came into being whose repertoire really was limited in this way. Serving for one round trip as a ship's musician on the New York run, I found myself in a quintet which had been sentenced, for no misdemeanour that any of its members knew of, to play nightly for the patrons of the first-class night club. We were not two hours out of Southampton Water before the five of us reached a decision. In order to make the time crawl less slowly, we would see how long we could continue playing the music each night of one selected composer. We worked at our lists, and on the home run actually succeeded in producing a whole night of Gershwin, another of Porter, and another of Kern, even though our performance was seriously impeded by the odd fact that our pianist, who had been press-ganged by a demented purser minutes before we sailed, had until that moment restricted his professional appearances to the saloon bar of a public house just outside Eastleigh. Each night we half-hoped that some discerning member of the audience, by which we meant someone who was still breathing, would approach the bandstand and say something to indicate that he had noticed what we were up to, but none ever did. Perhaps it was symbolic of the anarchic games we were playing on that trip that throughout the voyage home the elements flung our ship like a cork across the waters, causing the bass drum time and again to crash over the edge of the bandstand and go rolling like a juggernaut across the dance floor, where it would come to rest rocking gently to and fro against the tables, rattling as it did so with the noise of the contraband stuffed inside it. Magically the storm endowed smoked salmon sandwiches with the ability to fly at the same time as it deprived those who carried the sandwiches of the ability to walk, and eventually causing almost the entire passenger list to retire behind closed cabin doors, until, by the time we were back within a few hours of Southampton Water the long lit corridors of the first-class quarters looked like a reconstruction of the *Marie Celeste* the morning after. But still we ground out our medleys, too intrigued now by our self-imposed task to bother about a minor detail like going down with all hands. While the plates flew across the galley and the cutlery dropped soundlessly on to the carpeted fringes of the night-club floor, while silent waiters laid the tables with cloths dampened to hold the glasses, we presented our résumés of Gershwin and company, watched only by a couple of drunken honeymooners, the kitchen-hands leaning against the galley doors, arms folded, legs braced against the storm, and a few social climbers who had sneaked in from the tourist deck.

If that bizarre audience was ignorant of the nature of our repertoire, who can blame it when the jazz and musical comedy worlds themselves often betray the same ignorance? There is the well-known story of the trumpeter Oran Hot-Lips Page announcing to his club audience that in honour of the great Cole Porter, sitting over there at that table, it would give him great pleasure to play one of Mr Porter's best-loved songs, at which he then proceeded to play two rousing choruses of George Gershwin's 'Embraceable You'. A view from the other side was once given in a *New Yorker* profile on Porter, which included the hair-raising claim,

'Some of the swing boys are inclined to pout at Porter's musical tricks as compared to their own.' Even if we agree to overlook the fact that a writer whose experience embraces the extraordinary apparition of pouting swing boys is not one to inspire a reader's confidence, it still has to be said that the statement is not so much false as senseless, and it is senseless because the true relationship between songwriters like Porter and the jazzmen who sometimes use his songs as a point of departure has not been perceived. Only when the nature of that relationship is appreciated does it become clear why there should have existed so strong a link between what might appear at first glance to be two unconnected musical forms.

The jazz musician is someone who, by definition, is not concerned with the published melody. On the contrary, he is only in business at all because he presumes the ability to create superior melodies of his own. His concern is not with the melody which a Cole Porter might produce, but with the harmonies underlying that melody. The sole currency in which the jazz soloist deals is harmony. Harmony is his job, his profession, his vocation, his one abiding interest. The jazz art is the art of creating melodic variations based on an existing harmonic structure, and so it follows with the inevitability of truism that, so far as the jazz soloist is concerned, the most interesting composers must be those whose harmonic sequences are the most favourably constructed with a view to improvisation. It was therefore inevitable that the moment the jazz soloist perceived the complexity of Kern's harmonic legerdemain, the apparently endless harmonic resource of Gershwin's mind, the stark originality of some of Irving Berlin's inspired guesses, then all these writers should be drawn into a world of which they had no knowledge. Ira Gershwin once remarked in a letter to me that 'at one time I thought jazz meant absolute improvisation on the melody of a song'. The truth is that the melody doesn't come into it. By substituting the word 'harmony' for 'melody' in Mr Gershwin's statement, we can arrive at an extremely useful working definition of jazz.

For this reason, that the jazz musician has usually relied on the musical comedy composers to supply him with a high proportion of his raw material, it is understandable, perhaps even inevitable, that the apprentice musician, who began by learning Lester Young's solo recording of 'Lady Be Good' parrot-fashion, should have found himself twenty years later watching the London revival of the show for which that most durable of jazz themes had originally been composed.

GERSHWIN ON STAGE

In 1926, just about the time *Lady Be Good* was having its London première, the critic Carl Van Vechten advised George Gershwin to abandon the crass plot conventions of musical comedy and give his music a better chance of survival. The composer agreed in theory, then continued to accept those conventions for most of his short life.

Both men were right. Vechten lived to see 'Porgy and Bess', while Gershwin's confidence in the durability of his Broadway scores is still being justified. That Gershwin knew exactly what he was doing is proved yet again by the revival of 'Lady Be Good' at the Saville, where not even the cheap clichés of plot and characterisation, nor even indifferent singing, can detract from the tremendous vitality of the score.

'Lady Be Good' was the first of the Gershwin brothers' musicals and its shows their professional origins quite clearly. The structure is not really a structure at all, so much as a series of vaudeville sketches pasted together with climactic dance routines and comedy interludes. The fact that Lionel Blair and company are laughing at, rather than with, the farrago of missing heirs and mistaken identities doesn't prove that times have changed.

On the contrary, it proves they haven't. The original 1924 principals realised that 'Lady Be Good' was a witless charade, but they knew as well as Gershwin that this was an event redeemed by the music. Fred Astaire, who created the role of Dick Trevor, is said to have recoiled in horror when first shown the book, and to have changed his mind the moment somebody played the score to him.

That score is not quite the same as the one at the Saville. It has been buttressed by plums from at least three later Gershwin works, including 'I've Got a Crush on You', sadly crucified by a clumsy comic treatment. 'Fascinating Rhythm' and the title song sound as original as they always did, and for once a London pit orchestra plays with the kind of animation that Gershwin would have approved.

If the show does have a style, it could be defined as yacht-club baroque, with Blair himself managing to invest his hero worshipping impersonation of Fred Astaire with a kind of daft integrity of its own. Aimi Macdonald transforms the original Adèle Astaire character into a dizzy blonde, and Joe Baker squeezes laughs out of some amended jokes.

The only really relevant complaint is that although songs from other shows have been put in, one of the original numbers has been left out. Had the production included 'The Man I Love', originally written for 'Lady Be Good' and then discarded, it would have possessed one of the masterpieces of the popular song form. But even without it, the present company can claim to be working the best musical score to be found on any stage in this country today.

GERSHWIN ON RECORD 1967
TOP OF THE POPS

Ever since the death of George Gershwin, thirty years ago this month, the crazed world of popular music has never stopped pretending that his work has been outmoded by the new men. The fiction is probably necessary for the morale of Tin Pan Alley and the musical theatre, and is only shown to be moronic on the appearance of albums like *The Gershwin Years*, which reviews the entire Gershwin output from 'Swanee' to 'Our Love is Here to Stay'.

The exercise was worth doing, if only because so many improvisers have obscured the beautiful outlines of the original melodies for their own purposes. 'The Gershwin Years' attempts with complete success to restore the Gershwin songs to the settings for which they were originally intended.

In his nineteen musical comedy scores Gershwin extended the range of the popular song so wittily that even the Bernsteins and Loessers of our own day seem pygmies by comparison. Constricted as he was by the infantile plot conventions of his age, Gershwin nevertheless contrived to bring high musical intelligence to the workings of the popular song. Apart from indulgences like lampoon ('Strike Up The Band') and pastiche ('By Strauss'), he proved once and for all that the common herd will digest good musicianship if only it is given the chance, and it is this achievement which makes Gershwin the most important artist that popular music has so far produced.

Some idea of what he had to contend with at the hands

of demented librettists and megalomaniac producers is conveyed by the fact that one of the most exquisite songs in 'The Gershwin Years' and perhaps his masterpiece, 'The Man I Love', was ejected from three Broadway productions and eventually found its way into the standard repertoire only through the perception of musicians and cabaret singers. 'The Man I Love' has yet to be crowned with the full thesis its brilliant construction deserves, but 'The Gershwin Years' version may serve to remind the amateur musicologists of our own era that popular songs were not always untidy bundles of feeble clichés.

The modern listener, caught off guard by the purity of the four voices in 'The Gershwin Years' and the conventionality of the accompaniments, may be tempted to smile at the innocence of it all, but the smile should be wiped off his face when he hears the verse to 'Isn't It a Pity' and the choruses of 'Soon', 'I've Got a Crush on You', 'How Long Has This Been Going On?' and a dozen others. All these songs have virtually been banished from the popular repertoire by masters of the three-chord trick whose techniques are not up to the challenge which Gershwin's music presents. For a revival album to justify its existence it must preserve virtues which might not otherwise survive. 'The Gershwin Years' does this with a vengeance, and will be a reminder to all who hear it that the entrepreneurs of the 1960s have much to answer for.

ON GERSHWIN 1963
Gershwin. By Robert Payne (Robert Hale, 16s).

There was a huge split down the middle of George Gershwin's personality which makes writing about him an immensely difficult task. For all his dominance over the Broadway stage, Gershwin was a Liszt manqué with an ego so colossal that he had no trouble seeing himself in the long perspective of musical tradition. Usually the Gershwin biographer either builds a thesis around the amorphous structure of 'Rhapsody in Blue' and the lesser academic works, or he eulogises the popular songs. In either case he had better have a working knowledge of harmonic theory and the mechanics of composition, because Gershwin's true greatness lies buried in the harmonic progressions of his best songs.

Mr Payne, in going for the City Slicker aspect of Gershwin, seems rather to have missed the point about his subject, who was a popular songwriter of genius, a formal composer of inadequate technique, but above all a tough professional for whom music was an endless challenge inspired by visions of a princely bank balance rather than the rhythms of city life.

Mr Payne selects as his underlying theme the pervading Jewishness of Gershwin's music, borrowing Constant Lambert's specious theory that the Swanees and the Dixies of the early Gershwin were sublimations of the mythical Jewish homeland. Had he examined a little more closely the effervescence of Gershwin's harmonic wit, he might have been inclined to acknowledge more emphatically the strong negroid-jazz influence which colours Gershwin's best writing.

Prodigious natural gifts made Gershwin capable of a range which dwarfed all his Broadway rivals. He could move from the mock-Viennese of 'By Strauss' to the mocking American of 'Strike Up the Band' without the slightest difficulty, and his ability to concoct fresh popular melodies seems to have been inexhaustible. Whether he would have acquired the self-discpline necessary to his ambitions as a formal composer we will never know, but the author makes a point when he implies that 'Porgy and Bess', Gershwin's last major work, was more profound than anything preceding it.

The musicologist will find little to interest him in the text, but whoever writes the definitive Gershwin biography will find a few succulent morsels, namely that Gershwin was a proficient saxophonist, that he was what Mr Payne calls an impressive 'sexual athlete', and that the operation for the removal of a brain tumour, even had it been successful, might have reduced its victim to idiocy.

After reading this book, and indeed all books about George Gershwin, one is baffled by the enigma of his music. His orchestral limitations were obvious, there was a certain artistic fecklessness which Mr Payne rightly draws attention to, and a curious mixture of extreme arrogance and ruthless self-criticism. And yet the famous theme from 'Rhapsody in Blue', with its unmistakable overtones of Tchaikovsky, is probably the most familiar formal theme written in this century.

COLE PORTER 1966
JAZZ

The myth that Cole Porter never wrote a bad song is nicely balanced by intimations at the Criterion Theatre that he never wrote a good one. *The Decline and Fall of the Entire World as Seen Through the Eyes of Cole Porter,* hopefully defined by its deviser Ben Bagley as a 'revuesical', is no more than a ragbag of Porter songs which were either deservedly eclipsed by his real successes, or withheld from publication by Porter himself, presumably on the ground of poor quality.

Mr Bagley, something of an unsung hero in the campaign to restore neglected musical comedy gems, has made the revealing mistake of assuming that any song by a great composer is a great song. 'Decline and Fall', on the other hand, contains hardly a bar of distinguished melody and reveals that much of the humour of Porter's lesser lyrics has dated rather badly leaving an embarrassing residue of precocious rhyme schemes and empty virtuosity.

The songs, strung together by the most tenuous sociological links, are correlated by a spoken commentary so fatuous that worse could not have been done had the intent been to send up the whole Broadway convention. The archness of the script finally becomes excruciating when we are told that although Porter inherited $7 million from his grandfather when still a young man, he managed to overcome this severe handicap and write outstanding music. In view of the legacy it seems pointless to then be told, more than once, in pietistic tones, that Porter was a 'free spirit'.

An evening of this kind of Porter's music – or Gershwin's, or Kern's – might be made to work, but only if some reference is made to the context from which the songs have been dragged. And even then, due care and attention must be paid to details like singing in tune and at the correct tempo. 'Decline and Fall' ends with a medley of the more famous Porter songs; but four bars of 'My Heart Belongs to Daddy', followed by a couplet or two from 'What Is This Thing Called Love', and little more than the title of 'Begin the Beguine', is perhaps worse than nothing. There is a brief glimpse of that consummate distillation of the medical dictionary, 'The Physician', but taken at roughly twice the pace at which Gertrude Lawrence originally sang it, the wit sinks without trace.

The cast of five does what it can. Joan Heal has one sublime moment as a drunken chorus girl who arrives each time two bars behind the rest, and there is a refreshing slowing down of pace when Barbara Evans sings 'Experiment'. There is also a fragment about a pregnant ship's captain which Bill Oddie milks very cleverly for laughs, and Travis Hudson devastatingly lampoons Sophie Tucker. But it is a sad shock to learn that much of Porter's sophistication was mere name-dropping.

ALVIN AILEY
SONG AND DANCE

The key to the approach of the *Alvin Ailey Dance Theatre* – which has just arrived in London at the Shaftesbury – can be found in the list of battle honours of its leader. Ailey has studied with Martha Graham, danced for Harry Belafonte, choreographed for touring musicals, acted for the Theatre Guild, and the repertoire of his company reflects all these influences.

The tonal effect is one of movement and gaiety rather than balletic subtlety. What makes Ailey's group so easy on the eye is the way its work is coloured by the conventions of stylised showbiz New Orleans. The ladies flutter their fans and twirl their scarlet parasols, and the men pay court like Americanised apaches with inferiority complexes.

In his programme note, Ailey claims to bring us 'the exuberance of jazz'. It is a dangerous claim made good at least once, when Ailey himself dances an exquisite solo revealing the surprising balletic possibilities in Duke Ellington's little-known fragment. 'Reflections in D'. Wisely the company uses for this scene a tape recording of Ellington's own piano solo, which underlines the deafening obtuseness of the rhythm trio providing the rest of the musical accompaniment. Even the dusky resonance of Brother John Sellers, singing his traditonal blues from the orchestra pit, is drowned by the thumping and the twanging.

While Ailey used the prism of jazz to illuminate the dance, the *Black Nativity* company at the Vaudeville uses it to bowdlerise the Bible. By linking a series of spirituals with Langston Hughes's commentary, the company achieves a kind of syncopated Christianity which comes off because of the astonishing vocal gymnastics of Marion Williams, whose chubby face is repeatedly lit by the ecstatic smile of the true believer.

Both she and Brother Joe May are perfect examples of the link between today's jazz and the old Church roots, and the first half of their programme, 'The Child Is Born', is an ideal way to introduce a child to the story of Jesus. So much for the old view that the origins of jazz are steeped in lechery.

Virtuosi

WEBB, LUNCEFORD AND CO 1968

Among the more pointed jokes of the jazz world is the one about the agent who finds a Salvation Army group playing on a street corner and decides that the big bands are on their way back. They have, in fact, been coming back ever since they went away twenty years ago, and so far their return has been purely imaginary. Certainly the large jazz orchestras will never again be as numerous as they were in the 1930s, when for a whole decade dozens of them contrived to maintain the delicate balance between creativity and commercial appeal. By far the best of them, of course, were led by Ellington and Basie, but it has always been a truism of jazz history that those two professional survivors represented the apex of a very broad pyramid.

Probably the best two big bands of the period after Ellington and Basie were those led by Chick Webb and Jimmie Lunceford, neither of whom had too much luck in the popularity stakes. In *Rhythm is our Business* the Lunceford band plays twelve tracks, showing a power, resilience and melodic intelligence by no means rendered comical by the years between. In *The Golden Years* the Webb band, so feared by its rivals, displays the identical qualities in sixteen performances, including the theme which lent a kind of immortality both to Webb himself and the ballroom which employed him, 'Stomping at the Savoy'. Perhaps a clue to the felicity of the crisp ensembles of both these bands can be found in their excellent drumming, for Lunceford by James Crawford, for the Webb band by the leader himself.

Webb died at the height of the big band period in 1939, when he was only thirty-two, and had Woody Herman suffered the same fate probably nobody would remember him today. The most remarkable thing about his *The Band that Plays the Blues* is its tameness compared to the supreme brilliance of later Herman bands. The Herman Herds of the late 1940s threw up whole clusters of gifted soloists and revolutionised the shape and sound of the saxophone section, but the turgid blues of this original Herman band give not the slightest hint of the greatness to come, and are interesting only because they represent one of the most dramatic false starts in jazz history.

Charlie Barnet's *Skyliner* sees this same tradition in its decline. Barnet, a saxophonist who devoted his father's millions to the impossible task of trying to turn himself into Duke Ellington, was one of the last darlings of the ballrooms, and although the well-drilled ensembles of 'Washington Whirligig' and the title-track were cleverly deployed by ingenious orchestrators, most of the excitement, to say nothing of the jitterbugs who were bowled over by it, has melted away.

It is interesting that the degree to which all these bands have stood the test of time is connected closely to the ability of the individual soloists and the amount of freedom their leaders gave them. Ellington pandered to his, Webb and Lunceford appreciated theirs, Barnet gave his an occasional nod and took the process almost to the length of Glenn Miller, who by neglecting them completely produced the music which was different in kind.

The irony, of course, is that the big band in jazz began only because soloists were curious about the effects they might be able to produce in strength. *The Chocolate Dandies* covers the years 1928–33, when pioneer orchestrator-soloists like Don Redman and Benny Carter were experimenting with the then obscure art of scoring for sections. As early as 1928 the Dandies could produce in an Ellington theme like 'Birmingham Breakdown' that unique tension which only the interplay between sections could create. From these unpretentious beginnings to the smooth decadence of Barnet runs a process of technical advance at the expense of individual personality, but artistically at least, the large orchestra in jazz was able to enjoy a riotously happy ending.

Johnny Come Lately (RCA RD 7888) shows how the Duke Ellington band of the mid-1940s resolved every problem, managing somehow to produce ensembles whose wonderful subtlety never restricted the range of the gifted musicians who comprised its parts. The most remarkable of the sixteen tracks is probably 'Caravan', where the melody, clothed in the most ravishing harmonies, dominates without ever seeming quite to be stated. It is quite certain that neither Webb, Lunceford nor any of the other groups of the period would ever have presumed to measure themselves against music of this stature.

SIDNEY BECHET 1965

The established jazz master who frets at the senseless un-availability of his recorded masterpieces has at his disposal one simple and effective remedy. This consists of dropping dead, at which the world at large will immediately doff its cap with one hand and offer a memorial album with the other. The latest of these posthumous tributes has the for-bidding title, *Sidney Bechet – In Memoriam.*

Now the use of such a pietistic title suggests that the album consists of extracts gathered from a life's work ranging over fifty years. In fact it is something very much lese ambitious, merely the recollection of an afternoon in 1940 when Bechet, abetted by the cornetist Muggsy Spanier, contrived to record eight themes supported only by guitar and string bass.

But if the album is no comprehensive anthology it is a very good jazz record. Bechet was one of those musicians with a talent so generous that built into every phrase was the implication of a full rhythm section. All the greatest jazzmen possess this rhythmic self-sufficiency, and, oddly enough, Bechet possessed it more on one instrument than he did on another.

On the Spanier session, Bechet played clarinet as well as saxophone, but whereas on the latter instrument he was unique and virtually infallible, he was just one of many New Orleans clarinettists, and hardly the best. His tone in the lower register often sounds as though he were wrestling with the damnation of a waterlogged reed. On the soprano saxo-phone he was quite another proposition, soaring benignly over all technical problems, creating jazz so compulsive and so exhilarating, so finely executed and so emotionally frank that he can even be embarrassing to those raised on the intro-spection of the lesser modernists. He was particularly partial to the chord of the major seventh, a chord whose sentimental connotations have caused it to be shunned by younger men, but whose bravura sweep was ideally suited to the in-candescence of Bechet's style. On 'Lazy River' he demon-strates this appeal at a slower tempo, but it is on 'China Boy' that he dazzles the listener with the unimpeded flow of his thought, both in his own solo and in his duet with the cornet, where the sublimity of his impromptu counterpoint makes it very clear why moderns like Charlie Parker accepted him as a master.

He wore better than almost anybody else of his period, much better, for instance, than the instrumentalists on *Jimmie Rushing and the Smith Girls,* on which Rushing sings the repertoire of some of the women blues singers of the 1920s. Neither the clarinettist Buster Bailey, who worked with Bechet more than once, nor Coleman Hawkins, the tenor saxophonist who first delivered the instrument from the aura of bad music-hall jokes, possesses the spark of the old days.

THE LONELIEST MONK

After the shocks and surprises of the past year or two, it comes as a positive relief to discover that Thelonious Monk is still playing like Thelonious Monk instead of trying unsuccessfully to imitate much younger players. Monk's piano style becomes him. It has the same gentle eccentricities of his own nature, the same quiet confidence, the same inability to be false to itself.

The quartet Monk is leading for the rest of this month at Ronnie Scott's is not the most animated of groups. Its members do not excite one another very often, and the drumming is not as subtle as it might be. But in its leader and its tenor saxophonist, Charlie Rouse, it possesses two gifted musicians who have played together long enough to have achieved a rare telepathic communication.

Rouse is now in his twelfth year of unravelling the intricacies of Monk's harmonies, and is a past-master at resolving them into something poised and tuneful. He has an excellent technique and a clear light tone which provides the ideal counterweight to the heavy dissonances in Monk's left hand. But what is most striking about this interplay is the discipline lying behind it. Monk and Rouse are proving nightly that it is still possible to work within the accepted rules of the game and find enough freedom of movement to build interesting structures.

Monk himself remains one of the curiosities of jazz, one of its very few pianists who can make the instrument produce a personal sound. He belongs in no pigeonhole and yet is an unmistakable part of the evolving tradition of jazz piano.

Possibly the originality was forced on him by the limited technique of earlier years, but the important thing today is that he can do all he needs to. The key to his playing is the great tension between the deep inverted chords in the bass and the stark angular shapes in the treble. Monk's right-hand phrases are more remote from his bass fingers than the jazz ear is accustomed to, and they repeatedly stride across intervals we never quite expect. There is also a percussiveness about his touch which gives the end product great strength and resilience.

This is most noticeable when the group uses themes which ought to sound tired from over use. 'Sweet and Lovely' has that hint of diffidence which is usually an indication that the players have not been improvising on the theme together for very long. But it works because 'Sweet and Lovely' is made to take on quite a new personality. Here lies the justification for Monk's whole career. Not one of the great piano virtuosos, he has still contrived to make everything he plays sound like himself, which ought to be the aim of every jazz musician worthy of the name.

OSCAR PETERSON 1968

The jazz world of the moment is going through one of those tiresome periods when attitudes towards the music are considered more important than the music itself. It has happened before, of course, and no doubt in time the present phase will pass as all the previous ones did. But the current tendency has vital relevance to the work of a pianist like Oscar Peterson, now touring this country with his trio.

Peterson is probably the most accomplished piano technician since Art Tatum. Not even his detractors will argue with that. Instead they use his technical command as a stick to beat him with, calling him glib, mechanistic, unfeeling, etc. Recently a more serious charge has been levelled against him and many of his contemporaries. Having once been modernists, the musicians of Peterson's generation are now supposed to be reactionaries, presumably because in these days of nightly freak-outs, they retain their respect for the laws of harmony.

However, as jazz is not a political exercise but a musical craft, it may be as well to listen to what Peterson is playing instead of worrying about what he ought to be thinking. Because his groups in the past have remained unchanged in personnel for years on end, his present trio, only in its fourth year together, is looked on as a raw group which constantly suffers by comparison with its predecessors. In fact, the interplay between the three musicians and their concerted sense of time is not to be faulted. Sam Jones on bass and Bobby Durham on drums know enough about Peterson's approach to adjust to it, and the result is jazz of a very high class.

Inevitably the focus is on Peterson, and it is here that one sees the crassness of today's attitudes. For the listener able to dispel the morbid jazz tendency to dwell on a glorious and often mythical past, Peterson offers jazz piano of amazing depth and facility. As the years go by, a few more mannerisms creep into his work belonging to his great idol, Art Tatum, but now as always he remains his own man, making the old Tatum gambits sound quite different in a fresh context. And although it might seem like blasphemy to say so, Peterson has a more direct expression of the rhythmic pulse of a performance than Tatum had.

His repertoire includes two pearls from Richard Rodgers' youth, 'You Are Too Beautiful' and 'My Romance', and it is interesting that in the latter tune, Peterson changes its entire concept by increasing its tempo and approaching it as an aggressive jazz work rather than a sentimental ballad. And his version of 'Yesterday' is a lecture on how Lennon and McCartney should have handled their harmonies.

Peterson today stands as one of the greatest soloists of all time, a player whose technique never obscures the lucidity of his thought or the wonderful buoyancy of his execution. What Earl Hines began forty years ago with his discovery that the pianist's right hand was itself a solo instrument, reaches its final consummation in Peterson.

BUDDY RICH 1968

Drummers who lead their own orchestras are open to the same temptations as the old-time actor-managers who were more interested in a good part than a good play. The fact that Buddy Rich is probably the greatest drum technician jazz has ever known does not alter the case.

In theme after theme on his current concert tour it can be seen quite clearly that the orchestrations have been suitably phrased and broken up to fit the leader's style. The outcome is a sub-Basie group playing simply and crisply with lots of heavy accents made heavier by the punctuations of the leader. However, Rich is without question a special case who merits special consideration, and even those with no particular liking for ten-minute unaccompanied drum bombardments have to recognise his extraordinary virtuosity.

Rich has been involved in the big band game for so long now that it is child's play for him to phrase with his own ensemble. His movements are economical and his execution so crisp that the legions of local drummers who have been rushing to watch the Master have come away torn between ecstasy and despair. The accents crack out like rifle shots, lending animation to an orchestra which is competent rather than inspired.

Even on very slow pieces, where Rich confines himself to brushes, the cross-rhythms flicker quietly but firmly, tearing the listener's attention from whoever happens to be playing the solo. Each theme is introduced by a short drum solo setting the mood and tempo, and the general impression is of a house of cards held together only by the colossal talent of its owner.

There is something sad about all this. The days of the big band showman-drummer passed away with the end of the war, having reached their peak with the inspired antics of Gene Krupa, at that time every schoolboy's dream of the big bad jazzman. The fact that Rich does this sort of thing better than anyone before him is deeply ironic. This man, who displays so exquisite a sense of timing in his music, has been guilty of a serious lack of it in electing when to be born. On the strength of this kind of drumming twenty years ago Rich could have run for President. Today he is only a reminder of the old times. But what a reminder.

What would have been Rich's reaction, one wonders, to the drumming of the veteran Baby Dodds, whose first drumsticks are said to have been the legs of old kitchen-chairs? Dodds is one of several drummers who turn up in *The Blue Sidney Bechet*, their contrasting personas bearing witness to Bechet's ability to transcend all known pigeon-holes. Dodds is the drummer on 'Blues in Thirds', recorded in June 1940, only a month after Bechet had made 'One O'Clock Jump' with Kenny Clarke, the earliest pioneer of modern drumming.

Between Dodds and Clarke lie two generations of shifting styles, and yet both of them are blown into anonymity by the surging power of Bechet's soprano saxophone. Even the earliest performance on the album, 'I Found a New Baby', made in 1932, sees Bechet blowing with an assurance which demands comparison not with any other saxophonist, but with Louis Armstrong himself.

ERROLL GARNER 1967

When a jazz pianist commits himself indefinitely to a concert career, as Erroll Garner has done, and undertakes that career virtually unaccompanied, several of the rules of the game are bound in time to be displaced by new ones. At the Royal Festival Hall last Saturday it was clear that this is exactly what has happened to Garner over the last ten years.

Whether the mangling that jazz has endured in the process is worth it is another question, and the fact that right from the beginning Garner has been a freak, in the very best sense of the term, only makes the question more difficult to answer.

Garner is one of the great natural musicians of our time, a man with so intuitive a grasp of the mechanics of piano playing that he became a virtuoso without ever learning to read a note of music. He is also a prime example of the born jazzman, the instrumentalist to whom rhythmical improvisation comes so easily that it is no more vexing a problem than breathing or sleeping. The giant strength of his left hand makes the presence on the current tour of an accompanying drummer and strong bassist superfluous.

His choice of material reflects the reverence he feels for the very best popular composers. There are times when it is not Garner but Kern or Porter or Rodgers who seems to be topping the bill. Indeed, at one stage, during a marvellous Gershwin fantasia, Garner plays with such extraordinary bravura as to obliterate himself completely in favour of his material.

But what of the jazz world, which is too short of great musicians to be able to laugh it off when one of them absconds? Garner can still produce blinding jazz, and did so in London last week-end. But his concert career has tempted him into some dubious devices, none more suspect than his introductions. Before each song, instead of the normal rhythmic prelude to the melody, comes a strange fantasia of sound totally unrelated either to the pace or the mood of the piece to come. It all sounds like a wild pastiche of 'Dream of Olwen', the whole-tone scale and the collected works of Ravel and Debussy, and could easily pass for a lampoon of the 'con-shoito' that James Cagney's kid brother was always composing in pre-war gangster melodramas.

If this were mere sentimental indulgence on Garner's part it would be irritating enough, but it is something much more calculated. These introductions, being supine, create a tension which is suddenly released when the piano leaps without warning into the theme. The audience, spellbound by the hypnotic keyboard ramblings, is jerked rudely out of its rose-coloured reverie, realises that it is listening to 'Night and Day' or 'Where or When', and is so overcome with the shock of recogniton that it ruins the whole of the first chorus by applauding its own perceptiveness.

Garner is far too gifted to need such tomfoolery. The incisiveness of his touch and his ability to invent endless melodic variations should be enough for any audience, specialist or otherwise. Last Saturday he played a version of 'The Man I Love' so magnificent, that it explains why the jazz musician is sometimes obliged to coin new words and phrases to express his admiration for a fellow-performer.

ART TATUM 1966

The jazz world has never quite managed to make up its mind about Art Tatum. After all, must there not be some fundamental flaw in the playing of a musician who has intimidated everyone who has ever tried working with him? Apart from a few isolated albums, precious litle exists to show Tatum within the confines of the normal jazz group. Even the rhythm section, supposedly indispensable to the solo pianist, is quite unnecessary when he plays.

Faced with this awesome paradox, half the world's jazz critics have refused to acknowledge him as a jazzman at all. On the other hand, none of the great jazz pianists have ever dared to measure themselves against him. When forty-six pianists were asked to nominate their source of inspiration, thirty listed Tatum. Even the classical world blinked in amazement. Horowitz and Rachmaninoff are among the virtuosi who watched him at work and then confessed that what he was doing might safely be assumed as impossible.

Possibly the clue is Tatum's blindness. He had to manufacture a wholly subjective working method so that today the phrase 'a Tatum run' is an accepted part of jazz terminology. And perhaps that is where the trouble starts. Tatum has so much technique that it creates the illusion of a lost rhythmic pulse. He doubles the tempo and then doubles it again, so that the beat is convoluted, sometimes into un-recognisable shapes.

But those who insist that his tempo is unsteady always re-treat in disorder when faced with the inscrutable evidence of a metronome, whose steady ticking shows that Tatum is not guilty of varying his pace but is possessed of incredible powers of rhythmic variation.

Ten years ago he went into the Verve studios and knocked off a dozen long-playing albums in the time it would take any normal musician to produce as many single tracks. His material consisted of standard tunes, the hackneyed themes like 'Begin the Beguine' and 'Tenderly', and the lesser-known ones, 'When a Woman Loves a Man' and 'Ill Wind'. It was all like an after-hours recital, with Tatum moving from theme to theme with a nonchalance that suggests he could make palatable jazz out of any musical fragment in existence, which is probably true.

The richness of his music is too much for most of us. Tatum should be taken in small doses. The man who comes to him for the first time, after studying the piano playing of the Oscar Petersons and Thelonious Monks of this world is like a beer-drinker faced with his first brandy bottle. He soon becomes hopelessly drunk with Tatum's power. Any one of the new Tatum issues contains enough food for thought to keep a jazz-lover occupied for years. And at the end of it all, another fact is revealed which may have a great deal to do with the conspiracy of silence surrounding Tatum's achieve-ments.

The jazz world having been parcelled neatly into three independent packages, Trad, Mainstream and Modern, where do you put Tatum? In 1930 he was playing the same towns as Jelly Roll Morton and Fletcher Henderson, and yet using in his work ideas that are supposed to have been born over-night fifteen years later. The new releases were made in the era of Charlie Parker and the Modern Jazz Quartet, and yet the striding right-hand evokes wistful memories of James P. Johnson and Thomas Fats Waller.

The pigeon-hole was never built that could contain a player of Tatum's genius, and the only serious criticism left to answer is the grumble that right up to the day of his death in

1956 Tatum was becoming more florid with every performance. It is true that his style became too profuse at times, but
he never forgot the art of simple theme statement when the
melody justified it. His 1954 version of 'Lover Come Back to
Me' shows a musician so beguiled by the tune that he can
hardly bear to leave it for the customary improvisations. And
limiting himself to the stark exposure of Romberg's melody,
Tatum still sounds greater than any other jazz pianist of any
era.

BIRD 1966
IN PRAISE OF PARKER

During the 1940s the sound of jazz underwent a radical
change, and the end product of that turbulent period was
what is labelled today as modern jazz.

The figurehead of the revolution was the saxophonist
Charlie Parker, probably the most prolific improviser that
jazz has ever known. Without him there would have been
no modern jazz, and even without support he would have
changed the face of jazz single-handed.

The great paradox of Parker's jazz is that while he complicated it technically he simplified it emotionally. In the
Parker solo, no matter how profuse the phrases, or how
cunning the harmonies, there is the irresistible cry from the
heart which has always marked the work of the great jazzmen from Louis Armstrong on. Parker blowing the blues is
jazz so pure that even his lesser performances leave his
imitators floundering in the rear. Since his premature death
in 1955 at the age of thirty-five, a whole dynasty has been
built on his precepts, and disciples like Cannonball Adderley,
Sonny Stitt and Sonny Rollins have won wider acclaim than
Parker even dreamed of in his own lifetime.

But the depressing fact is that nobody has yet matched his
flair for melodic improvisation. Newcomers to jazz who know
of the imitators but not of the source may well be flabbergasted now by the effortless fluent grace of Parker's music
in this remarkable set of albums, some of which are available
to the British public for the first time.

His finest recordings are so sublime as to defy all comment. He seems to have been song-proof, band-proof, environ-
ment-proof. Norman Granz, who booked Parker for so many
outstanding recordings, and who is not the man to scatter
his praises carelessly, has said, 'Like any true genius, he was

ready to try anything.' What Granz means is made clear in some of the albums now appearing in specialist record shops. In every setting he soared above the rest of the company, casting a giant shadow over everybody who has had to follow him.

An illustration of Parker's greatness is to be found in the sides he made with violin-cello accompaniment. The string complement was sparse and the writing mediocre, and purists have suggested that the turgid background must have hamstrung the soloist. But in 'Just Friends' Parker plays the most astonishing solo, characterised by masterly technique and a tone of beauty and passion. It is the kind of jazz that most musicians can only dream about. To Parker it was a daily reality.

In choosing his themes, he would go to any source, from 'La Cucuracha' to Cole Porter. By moulding masterpieces out of tunes like 'Why Do I Love You', 'Slow Boat to China' and 'White Christmas' he established the current practice in the jazz world of drawing on Broadway for harmonic inspiration, but the essence of his art is to be found in hundreds of classic blues performances. 'Cool Blues', 'Now's The Time', 'Barbados' and 'Congo Blues' all convey his romantic power, the logic disciplining boundless imagination.

In Jack Gelber's 'The Connection' there is a character who wanders from pad to pad armed with a record player and one battered Charlie Parker recording, a talisman to protect him from the outside world. The motivation here is quite clear to anybody familiar with Parker's contribution to music. For thirty years the jazz world had dreamed of the perfect player, the soloist able to rise above all contingencies, the improviser who could pour himself into his music and justify once and for all the very existence of jazz. In Charlie Parker the jazz world found its man, a saxophonist whose music is illuminated by what Granz called 'great flashes of human beauty'. And because it is hard to imagine any phenomenon happening twice, it seems reasonable to suggest that Parker's recordings will never be matched.

BIRD 1968
Ever since the beginnings of modern jazz the art of Charlie Parker has posed the question to which there appears to be no answer. Was Parker's extraordinary conquest of chromatic

harmony the release of the music or its death-knell? Can a soloist have so much freedom that he gets lost in it?

Parker's ghost, in the form of his recordings, returns persistently to demand an answer. His memorial albums, five volumes of fiercely concentrated music, were made in the 1940s, first issued in this country in the 1950s, reissued in the 1960s, and now turn up yet again on the CBS Realm label as jazz staggers into the 1970s, perhaps the most crucial decade of its history.

The one thing which remains certain is that Parker's music has a grace and majesty unaffected either by shifting fashion or the process of maudlin deification which has been going on ever since his death in 1955. 'Parker's Mood', 'Now's the Time' and 'Billie's Bounce' remain three of the greatest blues performances of all time: 'Bird gets the Worm', a disguised version of 'Lover Come Back to Me', is still technically remarkable, even in these sophisticated times, and the 1945 Los Angeles Session qualifies as one of the key recordings of jazz history, as it catches Parker on the point of departure from the harmonic conventions of the past.

Putting aside the actual musical beauty of Parker's playing, one of the most interesting issues raised by the memorial albums is the hoary one of improvisation. The Parker issues were the first ever to present two, and sometimes three takes of the same theme, which means that Parker's methods of constructing a solo may be studied in detail. The sentimental belief that every time a jazzman plays he creates something unknown to him as well as to his audience has survived despite copious evidence to the contrary, witness Louis Armstrong's identical versions of 'Ain't Misbehavin'' over the years, Parker's two shots at 'Red Cross', with their identical structures, suggests that what really matters in the jazz solo is not improvisation but the preservation of its spirit, which of course Parker manages to do with no effort.

To sum up, these albums comprise a whole new vocabulary which has now served as standard language for modernists for twenty years. It was a colossal achievement which nobody but Armstrong before Parker had remotely approached, and which certainly nobody has approached since.

Whether its impact remains as great as it once was is doubtful. The daring neologisms have become clichés – the ironic fate of all successful revolutionaries – and the true force of Parker's music can be measured only if we forget about Sonny Stitt, Cannonball Adderley, Sonny Rollins, and countless others who have been working the Parker mine. It would have been interesting to know his reaction to the lions of the *avant-garde*, who pay lip-service to the legend even as they reject the inscrutable logic of his methods.

The Singer not the Song

There is no accounting for jazz singers, that is to say, singers who suffer from the dangerous delusion that they are jazz singers. I am not talking now about people like Louis Armstrong and Jack Teagarden, whose methods of vocal expression are so clearly extensions of their instrumental personalities, but of that curious group of non-playing singers, most of them women, who at most stages in the development of the music, have clung with such tenacity to the myth of their own jazz relevance as to occasionally convince other people. However, it remains sad but true that the number of non-playing singers sincerely respected by practising musicians remains so small as to be very nearly non-existent. The sincerity of these singers is of course unimpeachable, but then so was Genghis Khan's, and they remain a band of brave but deluded pilgrims marching resolutely in the wrong direction.

The reasons for this are obvious enough. The art of making jazz consists in creating melodic patterns based on a given harmonic foundation. It is an elusive and highly demanding art, extremely difficult to perform with any degree of subtlety, and the only known way of mastering even its rudiments is to spend ten or twenty years of instrumental practice, learning by trial and error how to play a game whose rules can never really be formulated. It is noticeable that this process is exclusively a musical one, and that lyrics play no part in it. In any case, if there are to be lyrics, whose must they be? Not those of the original lyricist, because once improvisation takes place, all the note pitches and note values to which the words were matched, are jettisoned and new pitches and values, those of the improvised melody, take their place. The utter impossibility of the situation becomes apparent the moment one tries to wed the words of a song to the improvised solo based on its harmonies, for instance the words of 'Body and Soul' with the new melodic line created by Coleman Hawkins in his monumental recording of that song. There is a further drawback, which is that while the improvised findings of the great jazz musicians are free of the responsibility to make explicit statements, the lyrics of many of their favourite vehicles are often trite to the brink of imbecility.

These are shocking handicaps, and over the years various attempts have been made to overcome them. Some singers have been so dense that the banality of the lyrics has never occurred to them, others so egocentric as to believe that the banality could be relieved by the amazing beauty of their voices. Still others have dropped the lyrics altogether and concentrated instead on making vocal noises which they hope with touching optimism will be construed as approximations of instrumental effects. One or two singers have even attempted to compose their own lyrics to existing fragments of improvisations, although they have usually been undone by the fact that there are in an improvised solo so many notes, and often so many notes within the compass of a single bar, that even the most clearly enunciated lyric tends to disappear in a blur of syllabic frenzy.

The truth of it is that there is no such thing as a jazz singer, which raises the awkward problem of people like Bessie Smith and Billie Holiday, whose jazz credentials are irrefutable. Their advent can only be described as fortuitous, a bonus for which our expectations must always have been nil. These two remarkable ladies represent two quite different lyric, though not jazz, traditions, Bessie Smith the uncompromising realism of the Blues, Billie Holiday the soft-centred escape from that realism so cunningly devised by Tin Pan Alley. In a sense, therefore, Billie Holiday's achievement is the greater of the two, for while Bessie Smith interpreted the poetry of the Blues, Billie contrived somehow to solidify that soft centre of the Moon-June syndrome, creating what poetry she could from a convention which had little regard for it.

Most of the jazz musicians I came to know well spoke to me at some time or another about which particular fragment of recorded jazz first impelled them to try making their own jazz, the first piece of music to offer them the categorical imperative of doing the thing for themselves. In some cases these primal sources might scandalise the purists. Indifferent big bands and inept small ones; three-chord tricksters from New Orleans and semi-commercial warblers who were not only devoid of jazz talent but didn't care. Of course it would all have been much more proper if every apprentice jazz musician had taken up his craft at the instigation of some respectable figure like Armstrong or Ellington or Parker, but the truth is that any old second-rater will do so long as he succeeds, however accidentally, in lighting the fire of ambition.

Billie Holiday was not the first great jazz musician whose work I enjoyed, but she was the first whose work brought home to me the injustice of neglect, and whose career taught me the simple truth that to be magnificently accomplished at something is no guarantee that people will ever realise it. A few girl singers I came across in my own career really did think that Billie Holiday was a man, but as they knew only the name and not the voice, that is hardly surprising. When I think of the vocalist who night after night sang

> You go to my head
> and you linger like a hunting refrain

when I remember the boy who ended 'Laura' with 'but she's only a fool', and after being told that the correct ending was 'but she's only a dream', compromised with 'but she's only a drool'; when I think of the girl who amended the phrase 'Creole babies with flashing eyes' to 'three old ladies with flashing eyes', was told of her error and then managed 'Creole baby with flashing eyes' and on being told that it was plural, ended up with 'Plural babies with flashing eyes', when I remember incidents such as these, I am amazed, not that there should have been so few competent jazz singers, but that there should have been any at all. And speaking as a worker who once sang 'Silver Dollar' to a ballroom audience in Dundee which responded by throwing pennies, I feel my competence to discuss the subject is not altogether spurious.

ANITA O'DAY

The exhibition of vocal dexterity by Miss Anita O'Day on the lawn of the Palace House, Beaulieu, last Sunday afternoon, is apparently the last such exhibition to be given at that charming venue. Lord Montagu, bowing gracefully in the face of the inevitable, which this year took the form of fits of drunkenness and a few bottle-throwing episodes outside the village local, has announced that there will be no Beaulieu Festival next year, or perhaps ever again.

It is fitting that the swansong of the Festival should have been sung by Anita O'Day of all artists, for her whole vocal approach is suffused with the wry sense of humour one needs to accept the gallant failure of his lordship to combat extra-musical vandalism. Her decision to include 'Sweet Georgia Brown' and 'Tea for Two' in her programme was more or less obligatory, for these were the tunes which in the film 'Jazz on a Summer's Day', introduced her to a far wider audience than she had ever previously known. A more eloquent testimony to her technique was her note-perfect 'Four Brothers', a famous saxophone instrumental whose chromatic conception makes it a daunting task indeed for any singer.

In the actual quality of her voice Miss O'Day cannot begin to compare with those whose recognition she shares. It is in its content rather than its vocal form that her style commends itself. As she plays capricious tricks with the time values and the duration of the syllables, it seems hard to believe she will ever succeed in fulfilling the one requirement a musician ever dares hope for from a singer, which is to finish at the same time as the orchestra. But Miss O'Day, who seems crazy, is really crazy like a fox, and achieved dead heat after dead heat with the Johnny Dankworth Orchestra with smiling unconcern.

Even more intriguing than Anita O'Day's mannerisms was the rumour that the scuffles in the village might have been between traditionalist and modern enthusiasts. It is gratifying to hear that there is anybody left in the country willing to fight for his artistic convictions, but the fact remains that the war between trads and mods, whether pugilistic or dialectic, is one in which the difference between the warring factions is quite imaginary. For a traditionalist to punch a modernist on the nose is about as sensible as Genesis declaring war on Leviticus because of its advanced position in the narrative pattern.

The trouble with functions like the Beaulieu Festival is that the social respectability of jazz is too new a phenomenon to be taken in their stride by its younger fringe followers. After the first stage, when jazz was besieged by the hordes of musical prejudice, came the second stage, still with us, of unlimited social freedom, which includes the freedom to commit mild acts of vandalism on the lawns of baronial estates.

One day, not too far distant, the reaction to the reaction will take place, and jazz will adjust its attitudes accordingly, neither tolerated as a novelty nor deified as a new source of musical godhead. Only then will organisers like Lord Montagu, whose heroic struggles to organise the Beaulieu Festival and his enlightened approach to selecting programmes were apparently for nothing, be able to organise their syncopated Salzburgs without fear of broken bottles in the bar parlour.

ELLA FITZGERALD

The two sides of Ella Fitzgerald's talent are almost never seen on the same concert, mainly because one of those sides depends for moral support on the presence of a large and highly spirited orchestra. For several years now we have been accustomed to seeing her presented against the background of a small group which is either extremely brilliant in its own right, like Oscar Peterson's, or the last word in tact and subtlety, like Tommy Flanagan's. The musical atmosphere engendered by this type of group is ideally suited to the lullaby voice in Ella, the voice which interprets the great standard songs so finely that not even their composers would be able to find the slightest fault.

But her all too brief current concert tour – which ends with London concerts at the New Victoria tonight and tomorrow – has the radically changed background of the full Count Basie orchestra playing with as much fire as we have heard for some seasons. The effect on Ella is to galvanise her into activity so violent that the more subtle nuances of the song readings are swept away in a riot of vocal improvisation which, because it casts lyrics to the winds, is the diametric opposite of her other, lullaby self. And while it is true that for a singer to mistake herself for a trumpet is a disastrous course of action, it has to be admitted that Ella's way with a chord sequence, her ability to coin her own melodic phrases, her sense of time, the speed with which her ear perceives harmonic changes, turns her Basie concerts into tightrope exhibitions of the most dazzling kind.

She does not, of course, abandon her other self entirely. There are still those moments when the hush of her own style induces a complementary hush in the audience. In her repertoire at present, along with three or four hundred other items, is 'Body and Soul', which she sings with respectful attention to the text and a unique blend of innocence and experience in the sound of the voice. And the quality of the accompaniment is so superb that throughout the song the entire Basie band can be seen watching the hands of accompanist Tommy Flanagan.

The scat-singing and the exchanges with the soloists in the Basie band are memorable for their technical wizardry. A moment like 'Body and Soul', on the other hand, is in itself a definition of the art of jazz singing. As for the Basie band, it is the same as always – that is to say, insolently at ease with any theme at any tempo, relaxed to an almost laughable degree, powerful when it cares to be, and hinting all the time at untapped resources, which is partly due to the fact that Basie persists in neglecting the solo talents of his rank and file.

By a lucky chance, Ella's concerts have coincided with the release of an album of hers from the days before Norman Granz gave her career the shape it should always have had. *Sweet and Hot* presents the kind of programme which was to become world-famous with the making of the Song-Book series, and reveals the danger of attempting definitive versions of standard themes, when the overall strategy is blurred. Among the composers represented are Rodgers, Gershwin, Romberg, Arlen and Vernon Duke and although neither their music nor Ella's interpretation has dated in the slightest, the orchestrations now possess a certain period charm whose effect is unfortunate.

RAY CHARLES 1968
To the seeker after good jazz attending a Ray Charles concert for the first time, there seems to be something wildly wrong from the opening bars.

The sixteen-piece orchestra which acts as curtain-raiser looks as though it ought to have the expertise of a Count Basie, or at the very least a Quincy Jones. One or two tenor saxophone solos almost justify this kind of optimism, but then the ensemble degenerates into ragged imprecision, a trumpet solo dies of self-induced strangulation, and the orchestra is revealed as a scratch unit lacking in either rehearsal time or professional skill or both.

What the performance has lacked so far in technique it

now makes up for in sheer senselessness. Charles himself, blind since childhood, is led on stage to the routine solemnities about being the greatest musical figure of the century, and then plays a short saxophone solo which proves that he isn't. He then sits at the piano and stays there for the rest of each concert, singing a programme of past successes, most of whose lyrics are undecipherable. To anyone unfamiliar with Charles's hit records, a Charles concert is like a *roman à clef* about which the reader knows absolutely nothing.

The songs themselves, most of which are Ray Charles compositions, abound in the kind of self-pity which expresses itself in lines about babies going away and people feeling lonesome. Once or twice the pathos of the Blues is achieved, but not often enough to sustain an evening of jazz. Charles has a voice whose rough edges are a sophistication of style rather than an inability to sing smoothly, and while the voice croaks on, Charles maintains an incessant barrage of rolling piano chords which distil into concise melodic phrases only once or twice an evening, giving a tantalising glimpse of the jazz pianist who lies half-buried under an inflated reputation.

Not till the closing stages does it suddenly become clear what has been going on. Four young ladies in white dresses march on stage with military precision. They gather round the central microphone, snap their fingers, sway their hips and make vague vocal noises. This is the masterstroke, the committing by a general of his last reserves, the assault calculated to induce the audience into the ultimate orgasm. What it did in fact do for me was to confirm what had been till now no more than a sneaking suspicion that the Ray Charles concerts are comedy shows and are meant to be comedy shows.

The four Raylettes, as they are billed, are among the funniest sights to be seen on any British stage, and they afford the vital clue as to what Ray Charles is up to. What we are seeing is not a jazz concert, although there are some interludes of good jazz. Neither is it a vocal recital, although now and then Charles does vocally recite. It is the old-time band show, a pre-war commonplace in variety, when a band buttressed its appeal by hiring a couple of singers and a knockabout comic. Judged by this criterion, Charles performs with admirable vigour and ability. Much thought has been given to the composition of his programme, and apart from the occasional orchestral slip-ups, everything goes according to a carefully laid plan. The only person likely to be dissatisfied is the jazz-lover who enters the house, hoping for jazz music and is so disenchanted by the time he leaves that it would come as no surprise to him if Charles ended the last number of the evening by firing himself from a cannon through the theatre roof.

BILLIE HOLIDAY 1965
At long last the definitive work of Billie Holiday has been made available in this country. A generation after the event, the achievement of this most remarkable of all jazz singers is made apparent once and for all. In *The Golden Years*, three volumes containing 48 three-minute performances show how the popular songs of the pre-war period could be invested with a depth of expression unsuspected by many of the composers responsible for them.

The plight of the jazz singer is unique. Unable to escape into the instrumentalist's world of abstract harmonic patterns, she is obliged to use verse that is frankly third-rate and sometimes much worse. That is why some of the most brilliant singers have been overwhelmed by the excrescences of literary style of which most lyrics are unfortunately guilty. It was Billie Holiday's gift to imbue triteness with profundity, and her success is all the more remarkable when it is remembered that public response at the time was minimal and the reaction of the recording companies something between indifference and contempt.

She triumphed through a happy combination of heredity and environment. Her father was one of the better guitarists of the 1920s, and although he appears in her autobiography only as a shadowy background figure, his daughter's life was saturated with jazz from childhood, with the recordings of Louis Armstrong and Bessie Smith as the primal influences – 'I got my manner from Bessie Smith and Louis Armstrong, honey. Wanted her feeling and Louis's style.' In a way she excelled both her models, for she never diluted her art for commercial considerations like Armstrong, and was rarely able to claim the support of the realist poetry of the Blues, as Bessie Smith had done.

She had, in fact, to create her own poetry out of raw material often pitifully inferior to Bessie Smith's repertoire, and she succceeded through a marvellous gift for phrasing, a perfect natural ear, and quirks of pronunciation by which instinctively she drew out the overtones of even the tiredest words. In 'Laughing at Life', recorded in 1940, the sheer exuberance of her style is so infectious that the song ceases to be a mere metric jingle and actually begins to embody the philosophy suggested by the title. It was absurd, but she did it time and time again.

Throughout her career she recorded with only the greatest jazz musicians, usually drawing on members of the Count Basie band, or, when they were unavailable, men from Duke Ellington's Orchestra, with Teddy Wilson an almost ever-present accompanist and Benny Goodman as an occasional member of the ensemble. Her finest recordings were pure improvisation, the musicians working out the background as they went along, and contributing in the process some of the most delightful solos in the entire range of recorded jazz.

The most amazing results of all came with her duets with the saxophonist Lester Young, a personal as well as professional friend. Young's languorous mannerisms undoubtedly influenced her style, and in 'Without Your Love', 'I'll Never Be the Same', and 'When a Woman Loves a Man' the voice and saxophone seem to strike up a telepathic understanding. No finer example exists of a performance growing out of itself than 'Without Your Love', where a casual background phrase of Young's flowers in the last chorus into a formal figure adopted by the whole ensemble.

When Young was absent, there were others in support, and the triple interplay between the voice, Bunny Berigan's trumpet and Artie Shaw's clarinet in two forgotten songs of the period, 'Did I Remember' and 'No Regrets', produced masterpieces of a kind subtly different from the antiphonies with Lester Young, more robust and rather less adventurous harmonically.

The thread of tragedy was woven into her life, and in later years the brave piping voice was to be replaced by the croak of a dying woman. That is why her career more than any other should be examined in strict chronological order. 'The Golden Years' sees her at the start, before the partial acceptance she later won, and before a chaotic private life made inroads on her technique. In the 1930s she was incomparable. It is hard to believe, even with the evidence of these recordings, that one woman's voice could be so exciting. She was one of the great jazz musicians.

1968

Most jazz groups look the same, and far too many of them sound the same, so when genuine uniqueness turns up it is something of an event. Anyone who drops into Ronnie Scott's Club in the next week will see some of the strangest goings on that have ever taken place in any of our jazz clubs. There you will find a small, bespectacled lady invoking the audience to look for Jesus, quoting chapter and verse from Corinthians and then laughing like a crone at her own piety.

Fascinating as this undoubtedly is, it is not quite enough to sustain a jazz evening, and this tiny demagogue is supported by four buxom ladies singing spirituals with such fiery passion that long before the end of the evening nobody would be very surprised if the Messiah turned up in the foyer.

The Stars of Faith are not quite new to British audiences. They have appeared in concerts here and were certainly more effective in the larger halls than they can ever be in the restricted space of a club. The success of their act depends very largely on the positive reactions of the audience, who are gradually browbeaten into clapping on the off beat while one or more members of the troupe passes among them daring them not to participate. It says much for the sheer animation of the Stars of Faith that even the most worldly of Scott's patrons end up shedding their inhibitions and stamping like customers at an old-fashioned revivalist meeting.

Not surprisingly, the repertoire of the Stars of Faith is musically naïve. The spirituals are built on the same few chords, the sentiments of the lyrics are relentlessly optimistic and all the melodies closely related. It is the professionalism of the act which carries it through. The four singing ladies are so familiar with their material that they could easily render it in their sleep, and probably sometimes do.

Their phrasing is as well co-ordinated as any instrumental groups, and the resonance of their voices is so overwhelming as to verge at peak moments on the comical. But nobody ever quite manages to laugh at the Stars of Faith. Their skill is too professional for that, and even the most fanatical atheist would be moved by the enormous volume of the voices, the generous vibratos, the fine enunciation of every syllable.

What is most interesting about the Stars of Faith is the way they demonstrate the close relationships, often forgotten today, between jazz and religion. Crossing the Jordan, going home to the Lord, and arriving in heaven, do not at first hearing seem like the kind of ambitions that have much to do with the jazz world, but take the vocal technique of the Stars of Faith, graft on to it more secular thoughts, and you arrive at that vocal blues tradition which has been the basis of everything that has ever happened in jazz.

Last Rites

In the late 1950s, when I first began composing the reviews comprising this volume, very few of us inside the jazz world had yet learned to live with the possibility that there might conceivably come a day when there would be no jazz and no jazz musicians to play it. Certainly the deaths during the 1950s of men like Art Tatum, Charlie Parker, Django Reinhardt, brought home the fact that one definition of the unique musician is that nothing remotely like him will ever appear again. But at least there was still Oscar Peterson, Sonny Stitt, Wes Montgomery. If great players were dying, other great players were maintaining the tradition. The idea had still to sink in that jazz, like the century which saw its rise, was approaching old age, and that the art of basing melodic variations on a given harmonic base might turn out in the end to be finite.

The appearance in 1956 of Miles Davis's 'Kind of Blue' was a straw in the wind so far as conventional jazzmaking techniques were concerned, and by the time the 1960s were under way, so was Ornette Coleman, with his creaky dialectic and meandering music. And while this assault against the castle was being mounted, those within its walls began dying off at an ever-increasing rate. The obituary columns were still short enough at the start of the period covered by this book to be novelties, long enough by the end of it to cause genuine fears as to the prospects for a jazz future.

It was obvious, for instance, that the death of Coleman Hawkins was rather more than the passing of a great saxophonist. Hawkins in his career encompassed more or less the complete history of jazz on his instrument. At the start of his playing life he had worked for Mamie Smith, and at the end of it his conception of how the instrument should sound was evidently still giving a figure like Sonny Rollins food for thought. With the death of Hawkins passed our last

chance to witness in the flesh the technique and the temperament of the jazz saxophone's founding father. If Pee-Wee
Russell was less significant, he was no less spectacular in
his way. He epitomised an era and an attitude long since
vanished, of unrefined, intuitive musicians with a limited
vocabularly, who nevertheless managed to produce the music
they wanted to produce. Russell was a representative of the
Chicagoans, that boisterous and fairly unsubtle bunch of
romantics who had in the end the choice of going for the
fleshpots, like Benny Goodman, or staying with their own
beginnings, like Russell. (It is very possible that the Russell
stay-putters were that way inclined, not because of ram-
pant aesthetic integrity, but because their peculiar techniques precluded them from ever subsiding into the conform-
ity of a saxophone section.) In any case, Russell, at the very
end of his life, had the laugh after all, in a most surprising
way. In his dotage he became a successful abstract painter
who sold his canvasses for far larger sums than ever he had
received for playing the clarinet.

If Sinatra's notice involved a man who although by no
means dead, had expressed a desire to lie down, the case
of Glenn Miller was much more unusual, of a man who,
although very dead, was refusing to lie down under any circumstances. Although from the jazz purist point of view
Miller is no more than a peripheral figure, like so many
peripheral figures he is useful in the way he defines the
boundaries of the art along which he so adeptly flitted for
most of his life. His orchestra marks the point at which the
diluting of the pure jazz spirit to suit the ends of ballroom
entrepreneurs caused the music itself to change form. Ellington and Basie ran jazz bands. Goodman and Dorsey ran
dance bands whose source of inspiration was the jazz talent
of many of the musicians comprising the groups. Miller ran
a dance band whose jazz content was virtually nil, and the
cynic is free to draw his own conclusions from the fact
that Miller, with the least jazz content, won the most public
support. But before dismissing him, it may be as well to remember that whenever he wanted a marketable idea, he
was inclined to borrow one from jazz.

As to his posthumous career, with its psychic junketings
and massed ranks of impersonators, one can only say that
he remains the only figure in the history of popular music
whose life after death has been maintained not by a ghost
but a regiment of ghosts. Shrewd marketing and a hard

core of fanatical support has had something to do with the phenomenon, but no amount of this kind of thing can ever create the kind of demand for a dead man's art that Miller has enjoyed There does indeed seem to be a genuine hunger for his music, and one assumes that this hunger will continue to assert itself at the box-office until the day when the last man who proposed to the strains of 'At Last' finally passes over into that conditon of nebulosity which Glenn Miller, all rumours to the contrary notwithstanding, has most certainly been enjoying ever since his plane disappeared over the English Channel so long ago.

PEE-WEE RUSSELL 1968

The death of Charles Ellsworth 'Pee-Wee' Russell at the age of sixty-two removes from the jazz scene one of the most puzzling oddballs in its history. Russell was a much-loved clarinettist of the Chicago school whose legendary reputation perhaps in the end outstripped his actual achievements. The trouble was that there was no way of knowing where technical ineptitude left off and gnarled originality began. Many of his solos were faltering affairs which often redeemed themselves from total collapse apparently by accident and always at the last moment.

The result of this bewildering tightrope act was that inside the jazz world, which has always been too ready to equate technical crudities with sincerity, Russell was elevated in his own lifetime to something between a genius and a talisman of the good old days. One possible explanation for his very remarkable and utterly original style, with its crabbed tone and vagaries of direction, may lie in his diffidence as a man. If this were so, it would go far to explain the often drastic improvement in Russell's performance the moment he subsided into the ensemble, where his experience and cunning left him very few superiors in the Dixieland jazz field.

A coterie figure content to be overshadowed by the shrewdly marketed virtuosity of contemporaries like Benny Goodman and Artie Shaw, Russell was one of the last active links with the mythical days when jazz was a dirty word and Capone was the musician's best friend. It was Russell who shared with Bix Beiderbecke the ownership of a broken-down Buick, whose front mirror never reflected anything more mobile than

Russell's own craggy face as he shaved each morning; Russell who was found living in a shack whose front porch was sagging under the weight of forty unopened quart bottles of milk; Russell almost alone of the Chicagoans who never trafficked with the commercial orchestras, where his eccentric tone would no doubt have been something of an embarrassment.

He also enjoyed what must surely be the most incongruous dying fall of any jazzman. In the last few years of his life he took to abstract painting and began receiving hundreds of dollars for his canvases. But it is an archetype from bootleg days that he will be remembered, and the recordings with Bud Freeman and Jack Teagarden that will preserve his reputation. He was probably at least half as good as the idolators said he was, which is really very good indeed.

FRANK SINATRA 1970

It will be some time before anyone knows whether Frank Sinatra's retirement will prove to be realistic or merely operatic, but there are certainly a few factors involved which make his announcement much more significant than most showbiz declarations of intent.

For one thing, it is extremely unlikely that Sinatra, even if he were to follow the precepts of one of his favourite lyrics and survive to 105, would have to make a comeback because he needed the money. Second, he is intellectually so far in advance of predecessors in his professional situation that there is no question of his ability to balance all the factors and arrive at a sophisticated decision. Again, in spite of the grandiloquence of his public statement this week, there is a chance that he is perfectly serious in his intention to read, write and teach. One book he should write, and is certainly capable of writing is an honest and literate musical autobiography. Nobody since Artie Shaw has attempted this, and nobody has such intimate knowledge over so wide a professional field as Sinatra.

From a purely musical point of view, his official retirement is an event of immense sadness. What few people apart from musicians have ever seemed to grasp is that he is not simply the best popular singer of his generation, a latter day Jolson or Crosby, but the culminating point in an evolutionary process which has refined the art of interpreting words set to music. Nor is there even the remotest possibility that he will have a successor. Sinatra was the result of a fusing of a set of historical circumstances which can never be repeated.

To sing as he does, a man would have to be saturated in a very special kind of musical environment, one which Sinatra was just in time to experience when he worked in the touring bands of Tommy Dorsey and Harry James at the tail end of the 1930s. Today the big band era is history, and there will be no more young singers learning the arts of phrasing and interpretation from the musicians supporting them.

One other factor may have helped Sinatra towards last week's decision. Last year I was discussing him with Johnny Mercer, a lyricist whose words have many times been given the definitive Sinatra treatment in 'That Old Black Magic', 'I Thought About You', 'I Remember You' and several others. Mercer said he thought the reason Sinatra had been singing so many new and occasionally inferior songs was not the desire to retain his hold on a younger audience but because 'he has recorded all the great standards at least twice over.' This is very nearly literally true, and, with his departure, popular music has lost its most powerful defender of artistic virtue in the recording studio.

GLENN MILLER 1970

In December 1944 a plane carrying Major Glenn Miller from England to France flew out over the English Channel, never to be seen again. And that should have been that. But the jazz world has always shown an odd weakness for the posthumous career.

For years after his death people discussed Bix Beiderbecke as though he had just gone out for some cigarettes and more recently the same was true of Charlie Parker ('Bird Lives'). Yet the Glenn Miller cult is different in kind. Bix and Bird were supreme creators. Miller was an indifferent trombonist who diluted the jazz tradition to become the most successful dance-band leader of his time. Today his work has only period quaintness to commend it, which explains a great deal.

The British Miller revival has been brewing for years, but

because it appeared to fly in the face of accepted opinion, the music business tried for a long time to pretend it was not happening. Today that is no longer possible. Imitating Glenn Miller has become a major industry.

The best and first of the copyists is the Syd Lawrence band, which began three years ago as an after-hours relaxation for the musicians, and has now snowballed to the point where the band hardly has a free night. *More Miller* is exactly what might be expected, faithful adherence to the sacred texts of 'Moonlight Serenade' and the rest of them. As a piece of impersonation it is ingenious, and obviously inspired by genuine respect for the original. But the degree of Lawrence's skill as an illusionist is less interesting than the larger issues it raises.

The theory goes that the big-band era is well and truly dead, that youngsters prefer the groups, that the old dancers are now pensionable arthritics, and that the jazz fan never took Miller all that seriously anyway. And yet Lawrence is drawing thousands of people every week. Evidently there is something wrong with the theories. According to Lawrence, he is attracting people too young to be smitten with nostalgia. And whether the band plays at concerts or in dance halls, the response is the same.

A clue to the mystery can be found in Volume 2 of 'More Miller', which treats the music of Miller's rivals, Tommy Dorsey, Charlie Barnet and others. Clearly what is being marketed is not just the music of one man, but of a whole era. And the demand seems widespread. Benny Goodman, who predates Miller, was flabbergasted last year when the band he took to Europe broke house records all over the Continent. Basie can do no wrong in this country, and it took Buddy Rich only two short tours to establish himself as box office insurance.

And yet nobody seriously believes in a big-band renaissance. What Lawrence's success indicates is not a demand for new bands, but access to the sounds of the old ones. It seems likely that the big-band sound of the 1940s will enter the general repertoire, to be produced when required, like the schottische or rock 'n' roll. And it seems to have occurred to nobody that the very ease with which Lawrence evokes Miller is an implied criticism of Miller's music. Significantly, nobody has yet attempted an impersonation of Duke Ellington.

In the meantime the danger of congestion grows. Lawrence produces echoes of Miller nightly. His rivals are holding their own concerts. And early next year the American version of the Miller band arrives for a British tour. Will the real Glenn Miller please stand up?

COLEMAN HAWKINS 1969

The recurring nightmare of the middle-aged jazz lover involves a world where all the elder statesmen of the music have at last disappeared, leaving only the young men in possession. That inevitable situation has now drawn one step closer, with the death in New York of Coleman Hawkins in his sixty-fifth year.

The jazz world may be excused for being utterly shattered by the event, even though Hawkins's physical appearance had telegraphed its coming for some years. Like Louis Armstrong and Duke Ellington, Hawkins has been a central figure for as long as there has been awareness of jazz as a method of making music, and, more than either of those two contemporaries, he could be said literally to have invented the instrument he played so sublimely, the tenor saxophone.

When Hawkins began as a teenager, the saxophone was little more than a vaudeville joke. He became the first man to lend it beauty of tone, coherence of thought, brilliance of execution. Recorded evidence suggests that it was around the late 1920s that the authentic Hawkins style finally matured. Before then his work, although scattered with hints of the grandeur to come, was still flawed by the angularity and the asthmatics of the early saxophonists. And then in 1929 with his famous recording of 'One Hour' it was suddenly clear to all that a classic jazz style had flowered.

Its features were easy enough to recognise: a rich ultra-romantic tone symbolising the phrase of the period 'hot jazz', cascades of arpeggios reflecting extreme harmonic sophistication, and above all that rarest of jazz virtues, a sense of form. When Hawkins played an extended solo, some intuitive gift made it possible for him to transmute bars and phrases into a single unified statement. The legendary version of 'Body and Soul', made in 1939, is as good an example as any, with its climaxes placed so exquisitely and its raw materials developed with such dazzling wit. When the listener grasps that this was a purely impromptu performance and that Hawkins claimed it was nothing special in his career, the architecture of the music becomes positively miraculous.

As a style setter Hawkins was challenged in the late 1930s by Lester Young, and perhaps superseded ten years later by Charlie Parker. But his influence has been so profound that there is literally no prominent saxophonist anywhere who does not owe him a vast debt. In his last years Hawkins became a far coarser player, yet, although the decline from the great years was dramatic, he still retained enough art to startle the listener from time to time. London had proof of this less than two years ago with his unaccompanied performances of 'September Song'. Beyond any question he will be remembered as one of the half-dozen instrumentalists who made possible the development of jazz.

LAST RITES
AND AFTER – 1969
Although we are only halfway round the course, there is already no doubt at all that the outstanding musical figure of 1969 is destined to be that Mrs Brown of Balham whose astral creativity is currently confounding the entire world of music. Mrs Brown's perfectly innocent remark that Liszt, Beethoven, Schubert and others drop in frequently to give her musical dictation has been received by the worldlings either with sneers of scepticism or what her spectral accomplices might have called hosannas of joy. The only thing that surprises me about all this is that anyone should find it in any way unusual.

After all, psychic manifestations are common enough in the world of music. Some years ago, when employed briefly with Lew Stone's Orchestra, I found myself working with a saxophonist who conversed regularly with the dear musical departed. There was also an orchestrator who swore that an extremely bitter heavenly feud was going on between Glenn Miller and Jelly Roll Morton, each of whom apparently felt that the other had been consigned to the wrong place.

So far as Mrs Brown's supernatural odyssey is concerned, I have no doubt that she is telling the truth as she knows it, that she does see and hear Liszt, and that she has indeed achieved every musician's ultimate ambition in becoming an instrument rather than an instrumentalist.

For the rest of us, we can only wonder why the giants have

waited so long to put in an appearance, and why they should have chosen this particular moment in what Santayana would have called sidereal time to do so.

It seems inescapable that if there were any logical moment for Liszt to have returned home, it would have been during the making of the film of his life, when he might have struck a shrewd blow for the Republic of Art by setting fire to Dirk Bogarde's cloak and planting mouse-traps in the studio piano. Still, if Mrs Brown is to believed, only now have the great composers seen fit to re-enter the game. I hardly dare think of the commotion going on in Valhalla at this moment of petulant creators jostling each other in the queue for Balham, of Bix Beiderbecke's concern whether he will be able to get a drink there, of George Gershwin's refusal to make the trip in case heaven won't be able to get along without him, of Paderewski's doubts about the strength of Mrs Brown's eminently suburban piano frame, of the certitude in Buddy Holly's mind that nothing he might do in Balham could possibly improve the already flourishing state of his posthumous career.

I now await the sequel to Mrs Brown's apotheosis, the return to terrestrial parts of the great writers. The re-appearance of Charles Dickens in particular would be most welcome, if only to resolve the question of whether Edmund Wilson or Felix Aylmer is right about the projected ending to *The Mystery of Edwin Drood*. But until Dickens does arrive, my thoughts about whether there is any cultural life on other planes yield pride of place to serious misgivings as to whether there is any on this one.

Avant Garde

In 1947 an uncle of mine, hearing me practising one morning in the attic of my grandfather's house, and becoming convinced by the experience that I was an undiscovered instrumental genius ready for the concert hall circuits of the world, attempted to expedite my progress towards the floral tributes and the standing ovations by arranging an audition for me with a friend of his youth who was now a nationally famous bandleader in a central London ballroom. It being understood that I was some kind of musical phenomenon who could actually play for ten consecutive minutes without falling over, my audition was not to be the usual private kind, but rather a baptism under fire. I was to sit in with this orchestra in the full public glare, at what used laughingly to be known in those quaint days as a tea-dance, taking my place in an unfamiliar ensemble, reading the parts at sight, integrating into the saxophone section by sheer instinct. As my professional expertise was minimal and my ensemble experience nil, I was of course in no position to perform any such feats, but some instinct told me that the fiasco before me was somehow vital to my future prospects, for I saw that only by enduring a long succession of such ordeals was I ever likely to arrive at any kind of professional ability at all.

But my feelings about this unsolicited gesture of nepotism were mixed. Certainly I was eager to play with other, more experienced musicians; certainly I was only too ready to relinquish belatedly my amateur status in a frankly mercenary world (I was now 20, and the whole thing was getting ridiculous). On the other hand, my critical faculties being far better developed than my instrumental ones, I was well aware that this fortunate bandleader before whom I was to display my tray of musical trinkets was perhaps the most execrable clarinettist still at large in England at that time. As for his band, it bore not the remotest resemblance to Count Basie's and therefore held no interest for me, I being too priggish by far at this time to see the absurdity of the comparison. As if this were not enough, there floated at the back of my mind the uneasy recollection of a remark my uncle had made to the effect that his bandleader friend never washed his feet or changed his socks. And to compound it all the date was August 28, Middlesex were batting against Northants at Lords, and Denis Compton, with fifteen centuries already to his credit that season, needed only one more to equal Jack Hobbs's records. Under circumstances so trying it is not surprising that on arrival at the ballroom I was too confused to know where to look for the tradesman's entrance, and ended up carrying my instrument case into the front foyer and paying for admission.

Soon I was shown into a tiny bandroom and told to wait till I was sent for. So I assembled my instrument and began warming up, drifting without realising it into Lester Young's solo from 'Dickie's Dream', which I had only recently succeeded in committing to memory. After I had been playing for a few minutes, revelling in the vicarious glory of Young's brilliant exposition of the use of the chord of the minor sixth, a small bespectacled man of about forty entered the room and stood nervously watching me. I stopped playing and he said, 'They're nearly ready for you. You'll see my chair, second one in from this side.' Then I noticed the saxophone sling round his neck and the corn on the thumb of his right hand and realised he must be the band's resident tenor saxophonist, the man who must by now be convinced that I coveted his job. I could see that although he was doing his best to muster a little of that professional camaraderie which is supposed to overcome all personal anxieties in such situations, but hardly ever does, he could not help revealing a certain blend of envy and worry in his remark to me, 'I can hear that you play this *avant garde* stuff.' And that was the first time in my life that I ever heard the phrase in normal conversation.

Modestly pleading guilty to the charge that I had indeed been playing *avant garde* music, and even more modestly omitting to add that I was incapable of playing anything else, I mumbled a few platitudes, not quite knowing how to convince him that I desired my escape from the premises even more passionately than he desired it. Then I shambled out of the room into the unnerving glare of the bandstand, to begin an audition whose course and eventual outcome drift far beyond the prescribed boundaries of this book. But the point of my story is to show how possible it once was for a trained professional musician to be confronted by the venerable harmonic practices of Lester Young and recoil from them as though from total anarchy. The modern reader may find such a reaction quaint enough to induce a certain complacency, but as he has absolutely no chance of remaining modern for very many years after reading these lines, he would be well advised not to become too complacent. *Avant garde* is not a style but an attitude towards Style; all a man has to do to backslide from the vanguard to the last ditch is to grow older, and so the jazz musician, if only he survives long enough, will find himself, much to his own amusement, having at various stages in his working life played not one but both of the roles in the bathetic little comedy which the bespectacled saxophonist and myself acted out exactly a quarter of a century ago.

But the reader, being happily free of the obligation of ingratiating himself in the eyes of bandleaders who never change their socks or their musical approach, will want to know who was right. Which of the two bigotries on display in that bandroom twenty-five years ago was justified, and what is more to the point, were either of them avoidable? The man whose job I was not after rejected Young's solo not simply because I might be a finer musician than he, but because the system of musical thought which made me better was beyond his experience, and therefore no better than malignant sorcery. Whereas he, no matter how hard he practised, would never sound like anything but a poor imitation of Bud Freeman, I would always sound like a poor imitation of Lester Young. It was the difference between the sensibilities of two eras. Perhaps to him Young's spectral minor sixths sounded like downright wrong notes, in exactly the same way as I myself was very soon to wonder whether the flattened fifths and ninths of the beboppers might not be wrong notes. Our respective ears belonged to successive and therefore to warring generations, and so there could be no common ground. With my neologisms he recognised he was being served notice to quit by the rising generation, and although for me it was the extremely serious business of art for art's sake while for him it meant nothing more than the frivolities of mortgage payments and three meals a day. I could not help feeling deeply sympathetic with his plight even at the time.

In the following record of my encounters with later *avant garde* movements the reader may think he sees the distance between myself and the performers increasing steadily as the years slip by. He may well be right. Just as my harmless second-hand minor sixths once alarmed a palais musician, so the innovations of later years have often outraged me, although I offer in mitigation of my own attitude the interesting truth that while my revolutionary gestures and those of the beboppers were still formal enough to answer to names like minor sixth and minor seventh, the anarchy of the 1960s, being totally committed, totally uncompromising anarchy, answers to no names at all, remaining free to make what noises it pleases, considerably alarming the natives in the process. But in Stevenson's 'The Beach of Falesa', the banjo strings in the tree being likewise free to make what noise they pleased, likewise alarmed the natives, without ever producing any coherent music. Whether or not present-day critics, chastened by the dreadful mess that was made with the entry of Charlie Parker, have quietly decided that it is safer never to condemn anything out of hand ever again I cannot say, but certainly in the years since I began reviewing, the streets have become positively congested with kings walking about with no clothes on.

For the record, I got to Lords later that day in time to see Compton bowled by Broderick for 85. It was another five days before Hobbs's mark was equalled, again at Lords, in the match against Lancashire. I do not seem to have been present on that day, and cannot imagine what kind of engagement it was that seemed important enough to keep me away at such a historic moment. Certainly not another audition.

1961

The myth that jazz is essentially a good-time music was finally laid to rest last week when the American trumpeter Miles Davis opened his long-awaited British tour. At the Gaumont, Hammersmith, Davis somehow managed to recreate, and even intensify, the hypnotic effect of recordings which have obliged us all to stop in our tracks and ask once again, What *is* jazz anyway?'

The power of Davis's originality is most effectively proved

by the astonishing way in which his playing places that of the rest of his quintet on a subordinate plane. His saxophonist, Sonny Stitt, prolific and irresistible, is an instrumentalist of immense culture and personality. It is hard to imagine even a partial eclipse of so dynamic an artist. But Davis, with a few notes selected with diabolonian cunning, forces us to examine the classical methods of players like Stitt from a new perspective.

The one very real dilemma of jazz music is the problem of the limitations of improvising on chord sequences. Within the framework of a harmonic progression the musician is free to trace whatever melodic patterns he can. But one senses, in the work of the most gifted soloists and in the fidgeting of younger rebels, a certain resigned acceptance of the theory that the utmost limits have almost been reached.

The attempt by Davis to solve this problem was admirably posed at Hammersmith by the sharp contrast between the material Davis first introduced on his albums, and the more orthodox themes which form perhaps half of the quintet's repertoire. Significantly, Miles opened and closed his first British concert with two themes from his 'Kind of Blue' recording, one which questioned the tenets of jazz-making more searchingly than anything since Charlie Parker. With those two themes, 'Freddie Freeloader' and 'All Blues', Davis cast a spell already familiar to those who know the recordings.

What is it about this spell which makes it so very different from any other jazz? To put it briefly, Davis has succeeded in introducing into the jazz context a new aesthetic. Every note he plays is tinged with the disturbing melancholia of a highly sophisticated and super-sensitive artist. Nowhere is there any trace of the unselfconscious joy at being alive of Louis Armstrong, or the irrepressible good spirits of Davis's great contemporary, Dizzy Gillespie. Suddenly, through the prism of Davis's conception, all other jazz appears a Panglossian affair concerned with the release of tension rather than the exploration of it. With Miles Davis, introspection enters the jazz world, and just as Lester Young, when he introduced the qualities of wit into the idiom, used new weapons, so Davis has been obliged gradually to evolve an approach of his own.

Tonally he has dramatically distilled the sound of the trumpet, so that it now possesses a deathly purity evoking all kinds of poetic images. Vibrato has almost disappeared completely, and forgotten is the old avowed intention of the instrumentalist to suggest the overtones of the human voice, still very apparent in contemporaries like Ellington's Clark Terry. When Miles, using a mute, improvises on 'Green Dolphin Street' and 'Round Midnight', he achieves a spectral evocation which makes even Lester Young's pre-war legerdemain sound like jolly extroversion. Were I limited to one adjective in reference to Miles Davis, I would probably settle for 'crepuscular'.

The 'Kind of Blue' material reflects Davis's attempt to escape from the cage of normal progression from discord to resolution without shattering the jazz form entirely. The themes are based less on chord progressions than on a series of modal scales, whose possibilities Davis probes with consummate delicacy, employing a more rigorous selection and economy of note than anybody before him. To find any parallel at all with this introversion I can think only of the piano fragments of Bix Beiderbecke thirty years before, although these were necessarily quite different in harmonic conception.

Davis's originality is underlined by Stitt when the group plays a conventional blues theme like 'Walkin'.' Here Stitt is positively brilliant, playing with masterly execution and producing a cascade of ideas completely overwhelming to the listener bred on a diet of derivative homegrown jazz. The contrast between Stitt and his leader serves also to remind us that Davis is limited by the very nature of his development to a single mood, but that within its confines he is one of the great jazzmen.

The presentation of this new approach has given rise to some touching confusion on the part of audiences. Davis says not a single word throughout his concerts. He makes no announcements and even leaves the stage when not actually playing. Some people have used this austerity as an excuse to talk of Miles Davis's 'failure to project' or even his bad professional manners. The truth is that Miles projects with his trumpet, and that his so-called snubbing of the audience is merely a flattering assumption that any audience which pays to see him knows enough about what is going on to be spared announcements of the 'For my next number' variety.

As for the benumbing jocosities of most jazz group leaders, Davis is quite justifiably contemptuous of such attempts to milk his followers. He is trying to invest a jazz performance with the same dignity and self-assurance which he himself possesses to such a remarkable degree. Those knockabout comics, the Modern Jazz Quartet, would do well to study him a little more closely. Rarely have I witnessed a more impressive concert of jazz.

1966

Judged by the normal jazz standards, Sonny Rollins is neither good, bad nor indifferent. This awkward fact was apparent within five minutes of this American virtuoso's arrival in London at Ronnie Scott's club last week-end.

Whatever he is trying to do with his saxophone, it no longer has much relation to what Coleman Hawkins or Lester Young or Charlie Parker were trying to do with theirs. There are moments when Rollins sounds so inept as to be embarrassing. There are moments when he sounds so gifted as to be terrifying. His playing is more uneven than any heard in this country, and it is quite clear that the usual considerations of good tone, fluency and melodic grace are placed far out of court when listening to him.

The dilemma of Rollins is the dilemma of jazz. How far can the improviser go in broadening his harmonic range? Today it is almost possible to play any note against any chord and justify its presence by some esoteric harmonic theory. Rollins ties himself up into such frightful knots at times that there is a temptation to dismiss him as a fake. But what of the recordings he made in the late 1950s, those fiery and beautifully lucid expositions of jazz art? No man who achieved that standard could possibly be a charlatan.

Ronnie Scott has already remarked that listening to Rollins at close quarters every night is like watching the history of jazz saxophone being unfolded, and it is true that there are times when the shadows of previous masters flicker across the face of a Rollins solo. He begins a blues, and the first four bars are a lovely lightning sketch of Lester Young. But then the likeness disappears and is usurped by a succession of difficult and often ugly intervals. Suddenly coherence returns with a masterly passage which Charlie Parker would have been proud of. Then the ungainliness returns as Rollins attempts to find his way.

About three years ago Rollins reached a crisis in his

affairs which very neatly symbolises the crisis of jazz itself. He retired from active combat and for more than a year was said to be thinking his way into a new approach. Since his comeback he has evidently conquered many of the conventional fears of the soloist.

There is no longer any inhibition. Unlike a Louis Armstrong, who panders to an audience, or a Miles Davis, who conducts a running war with it, Rollins simply takes no notice. He hardly sees the people sitting before him. He starts playing as he shoulders his way through the fans to the bandstand. During bass and drum solos he burbles quietly to himself, as though there was nobody else in the room. If a tune happens not to suit his mood he stops in the middle and sweeps into something else. He is unconcerned with the niceties of performance, and is quite unperturbed by the squeaks and grunts which mar the symmetry of even his most lucid moments.

Patently this kind of music is a different proposition to all the jazz that has gone before. Rollins is no mere modernist chord sharper, neither is he the moulder of neat 32-bar packages. It may well be that what he represents is jazz at the moment of dissolution, an art stretched to breaking point by sheer ingenuity.

Whatever the truth, the usual measuring rods are useless. The only man who might know what standards to judge by is Rollins himself, and even he has confessed his uncertainty. In the meantime his playing at Scott's is an extraordinary thing, a great rubbish dump sprinkled with exquisite pearls of wisdom.

1967

It ought to be clear to anyone visiting Ronnie Scott's club in the last few days that it is not possible to criticise the playing of Ornette Coleman. The act of criticism is necessarily connected with what the artist is supposed to be doing, and as I haven't the remotest idea what Ornette Coleman is supposed to be doing all criticism is stilled. It remains only to report in strict factual terms what happens when Coleman arrives on the bandstand with his supporting drummer and string bassist.

Coleman begins with what might laughingly be called an alto saxophone solo at a fast tempo, brief and to the point, lasting say ten or fifteen minutes, in the course of which both harmony and melody are given the brush. Next comes a change of mood, that is to say, the same thing is played slow instead of fast. The violin interlude which follows is even more startling. Coleman staggers through some mysterious pattern of his own devising, sawing away with a ferocity which belies the dolorous expression on his face.

Employees at the club, who will be privileged to witness this performance nightly for the next three weeks, swear to me that Coleman runs through three violin bows a week, and that at the end of each session the bandstand is strewn with mangled cat-gut.

Finally, there arrives what will probably come to be known in jazz history as Coleman's Trumpet Involuntary, in which this unique artist plays a series of strangulated bugle calls and high chromatic runs with a fine disregard for all present.

He is not, however, completely without shrewdness. By mastering the useful trick of playing the entire chromatic scale at any given moment, he has absolved himself from the charge of continuously playing wrong notes. Like a stopped clock, Coleman is right at least twice a day.

To me the most remarkable thing of all is the sycophancy of his audiences, who sit in awed silence throughout each number, and then applaud like a barbarian horde hailing the fall of a great city. Unquestionably Coleman is king of the *avant garde*, but I cannot help wondering how many people have noticed that he is wearing no clothes.

1968
MONEY FOR IMPROVISING

Whatever its merits or defects, Graham Collier's 'Work-points', being the first jazz work to be subsidised by an Arts Council bursary, deserves a footnote to the social history of the times. It would be gratifying to claim it as a masterpiece, except that everyone, Collier included, knows it is not. But the point is that a fifty-minute jazz work is now being performed which would not otherwise have existed, and Collier, aware of the significance that official patronage could hold for British jazz has struggled heroically to produce something worthy of the occasion.

The great difficulty here is that the true spirit of jazz is embodied in its soloists, and no official body is ever likely to subsidise a soloist. In 'Workpoints', however, improvisation plays so dominant a role that indirectly the soloist has indeed been supported by the bursary.

It is based on a slender theme which is stated briefly and then reshaped at length by a series of improvisations from the members of Collier's twelve-piece group. Reeds, brass and rhythm all take a turn with the thematic material, against a turbulent orchestral background which is itself semi-improvised. The result is often confusing, sometimes boring, and occasionally very stimulating indeed.

The degree to which any orchestra of this size can enjoy the freedom of improvisation is problematic. But Collier has attempted to solve the riddle by giving his musicians a choice of orchestral figures to play behind each soloist. The point about this kind of performance is that it becomes quite impossible without constant rehearsal and a high degree of understanding between the players, and it is partly this long, painstaking process that the bursary has been subsidising.

'Workpoints' may be summed up as a composition adventurous in form but conventional in procedure, even down to the long drum solo towards the end. For a long time now there has been growing in British jazz a strong groundswell of reaction against the old methods of improvisation, and it is a good thing that Collier has been given the chance to express this impatience in positive form with the help of a young skilful group, held together by the virile drumming of John Marshall.

1969

There have been some very strange goings-on in the jazz world over the last ten years, and most of them have come about because of the steady loss of faith by instrumentalists in the conventional methods of making music. In the welter of noise that has resulted, only a few of the experimentalists have been entirely above suspicion. The most significant was the late John Coltrane, whose earlier work, brilliant and profound, absolved him from any charges of charlatanism.

But something went seriously wrong with Coltrane in the 1960s. *Selflessness* seems to locate the crisis between the years 1963–65. It included his remake of 'My Favourite Things' (1963), when he still retained a firm grip on the material and his own approach to it. Yet there were strong hints even then that he was edging towards the kind of performance in which fast-moving harmonies are exchanged for a mere two or three chords repeated *ad nauseam*. Indeed, this may well be the reason why a tune like 'My Favourite Things' appealed to him. Nevertheless, in 1963 Coltrane's soprano saxophone playing (not tenor, as the sleeve note says) was still rooted in the traditions of jazz.

The title track of the album was recorded two years later, and in the intervening period he appears to have suffered some kind of a brainstorm. The music was now deliberately crude and discordant, and any pretence of form had finally vanished. 'Selflessness' is a destructive performance which presumably was no more than an incident on the road to a new kind of music, but Coltrane's premature death leaves us guessing what kind of music it might have been. It's likely that with his death went the *avant garde's* best chance of achieving some kind of coherence.

One of the side effects of this confused revolution has been to make what used to be ultra-modern sound comfortingly familiar. *The Best of Horace Silver* is a summary of small group jazz in the later 1950s and underlines once more the vital importance in jazz, as in all other music, of melodic invention. Silver has always had the knack of composing easily assimilated melodies which have a foundation of highly sophisticated harmonies, and themes like 'Senor Blues' and 'Filthy McNasty' have stood the test of time surprisingly well.

Silver, however, is very much more than a witty miniaturist. On all six tracks it is his own piano playing which stands out. Only in the face of very recent developments does it appear to have dated, and that, in the long run, may turn out to have been a good thing.

As for the really ancient jazz, this seems to come to us now across the gulf of several centuries. *Louis Armstrong in Los Angeles 1930* which includes the now classic versions of 'Shine', 'I'm Confessing', and 'One Hour', sounds positively mythological, and if the latest Django Reinhardt reissue *Django* is not quite as hypnotic, probably it is because it shows Reinhardt rather below his pre-war peak.

1970

Mike Westbrook's 'Earthrise' at the Mermaid Theatre is a work of the most amazing pretentiousness. It attempts, by combining the effects of a large jazz orchestra with those of lantern slides and flashing lights, to celebrate man's conquest of the moon as a theatrical experience. The orchestra stands before two large screens, while spotted about the building like snipers in strategic positions are shadowy figures manning things which go flash in the night.

The connection between the music, the moon and the slides is not always apparent. On the central screen it is El Greco one minute, Eugene Sandow the next, and we even catch a glimpse of an Edwardian music-hall artist called Patsy Montague, who used to bill herself as La Milo, the Living Statue, and was the toast of many a bar parlour.

Meanwhile on the other screen molecular shapes perform the dance of life with that depressing lack of imagination molecules always show in a crisis, looking suspiciously like clots of strawberry jam being pushed over a precipice. The orchestral ensemble is augmented by the voice of Norma Winstone whooping in the extreme upper registers, and the whole effect is overlaid by intrusions of reality like the voice of an astronaut or the sound of an air-raid siren. Chagall and Miró alternate with children's doodles, and through it all the band plays resolutely on, having taken the wise precaution of admitting in the programme that some of the music 'sounds wrong to our ears, but it has a mysterious logic of its own'.

The claim is not quite accurate. Westbrook is a common enough example of the young jazz musician torn between affection for the past and a desire to destroy it. His old-fashioned self, well in evidence in the earlier phases of 'Earthrise' derives from those quasi Latin American brass marathons of the old Stan Kenton band, except that the Westbrook version never quite achieves the vital ensemble cohesion. The music becomes blurred by the imprecision of the players, so that the effect is like looking at Kenton through the wrong end of a misty telescope. In the long run this will affect Westbrook less than the fact that his model is second-rate anyway. It may well be that he has been doing the wrong homework.

His other self is devoted to the freak-out, that pestilential device which encourages each musician to play what he pleases and dump on the audience the responsibility of discovering coherence. Until Westbrook decides whether he wants to produce noise or sound, his work will continue to show this schizoid tendency. Strongly in his favour is the fact that he has already grasped the principle that volume of sound submitted to a tight formal discipline can create tremendous tension and excitement, and there are a few moments in 'Earthrise' when he proves this.

At the one point when man arrives on moon, somebody hiding in the window of the building started flashing lights on and off in my face, so I took the hint and went home. Anybody who finds this sequence of events improbable can see for himself tonight at the Mermaid at 7.30 when Westbrook will be conquering the moon all over again.

Father Figures

From 1943 to 1948, a period which in retrospect I can see constituted my apprenticeship, all my contemporaries conducted fierce tribal wars in support of their chosen heroes. There was, for instance, a Benny Goodman camp and an Artie Shaw camp, a Tommy Dorsey set and a Harry James set, a Gene Krupa clique and a Charlie Christian lobby, while for comparative eclectics like myself there were such issues as Bix Beiderbecke or Muggsy Spanier, Fats Waller or Teddy Wilson, Bud Freeman or Coleman Hawkins. Generally the movement tended to be a progressive one, towards the giants of the Swing Age, the pathos of the debate being heightened by the fact that, unknown to us, the issues over which we squabbled were dead ones, for the Swing Age and all its heroes were already disappearing over the horizon. Of course there existed concurrently with our world several antiquarian sects whose members, mistaking the recorded ineptitude of some New Orleans pioneers for a musical style, tried inexplicably to reproduce it, with horrific results. However, as I encountered none of these sects, with their reverence for Baby Dodds's chairleg drumsticks and their confusion as to whether the Charleston Chasers ever caught anybody, until long after their excesses could appear anything but comic, I take no account of them in this reminiscence.

Although none of us yet suspected it, by acquiring Swing Age nuances which were already beginning to lose their relevance, we were creating awkward stylistic problems for ourselves in the future. I recall one trombonist who appeared for a while in one of the many amateur groups with which I became involved during those years. Always in these groups we would rehearse with manic fervour against the arrival of a yearned-for first engagement which was destined never to come, and this trombonist shocked us all by conducting an endless debate with himself over the relative merits of Miff Mole and Jack Teagarden. Our surprise was due to the fact that we credited him with a modernity which his style did nothing to confirm, although now I come to think of it he did possess a pair of rimless spectacles which endowed him with a certain superficial resemblance to Benny Goodman, Glenn Miller and Tommy Dorsey. I remember very clearly doing an audition for an extremely trendy semi-professional sextet whose method of testing my abilities was to confront me with the printed transcript of the Artie Shaw Gramercy Five recording of 'Special Delivery Stomp', complete with all the trite riffs and pointless chromatic excesses, my disapproval of such fripperies being quite unconnected with my total inability to play them. This was in 1945, when Shaw had already made several final appearances, and Charlie Parker was embarked on his quintet recordings with Dizzy Gillespie.

Presiding over this gently anachronistic world were two dominant figures, twin deities who did not feature in our disputations at all, Louis Armstrong and Duke Ellington. It would be comforting to pretend that the reason for their absence was that they were considered by us all to be beyond criticism. Unfortunately this would be quite untrue. As far as I remember, of all the dozens of clarinettists, electric guitarists, one-key boogie-woogie pianists and dixieland drummers who marched across the drawing-rooms and youth clubs halls of the period, not one was familiar with any Armstrong or Ellington recordings. As my own researches had begun, not along the usual route of the local palais and the big bands, but with the more esoteric deliberations of Bix Beiderbecke, it might be expected that I at least was acquainted with this vast body of utterly indispensable music. In fact, my ignorance was as unblemished as anyone else's. It is true that I had been familiar with the work of the Ellington small groups, with particular reference to Johnny Hodges, almost since I had first begun learning, but my interest abruptly ceased the moment such groups grew beyond eight pieces. So far as the full Ellington band was concerned, I agreed with all my contemporaries that it was no more than a glorified dance band whose integrity must be suspect because of the high proportion of orchestrated, notated music it played. As for Armstrong, it was too obvious for words that he was a New Orleans relic whose significance had faded with the years, and who had himself acknowledged the fact by turning to a career in Hollywood and Variety. The interesting thing about all this is that up to a point we were quite right. Ellington's *was* a glorified dance band. Armstrong *was* a professional comic. What the fierce bigotry of inexperience prevented us from conceding was the possibility that they might also be something more. It was not until long after I had come to take my own professional daily round for granted that I came to see this.

Armstrong's primacy was, of course, unavoidable. It impinged at too many points of jazz experience to be ignored. There was Bunny Berigan's 'I Can't Get Started', a brilliant and passionate composition – of Armstrong's phrases. There was the Goodman big band, sparked by the orchestrations of Fletcher Henderson – who had doubled the power of his own band by persuading Armstrong to join it. There was the beloved Chicagoan Jack Teagarden, who was rumoured to be working with Armstrong in an authentic jazz environment once more. There were those curious moments in movies where something Armstrong did made you tap your foot or catch your breath. There were the hundreds of testimonies from virtually every jazz musician of any stature, that Armstrong was supreme, that Armstrong had started it all, that Armstrong remained as powerful as ever, that jazz would never see a more completely equipped soloist, and so on. It finally became necessary to examine the evidence, if only to refute it. And then the truth began to emerge. Gradually I learned never to be surprised by anything Armstrong did. The last time he ever shocked me was in 1957, when I heard his album of Fats Waller themes, at a time when I had assumed him to be an ageing lion, too old to strike many more sparks. But his Waller album was one of the masterpieces of his life.

My introduction to the body of Ellington's music was altogether more bizarre. No doubt in time I would have discovered it for myself one way or another, which is to say that in time some more enlightened friend would have been sure to thrust it under my nose. But the actual circumstances are comic, and perhaps very faintly pathetic. One day in 1952 a fellow-saxophonist called Klein, one of the wisest of musicians and most loyal of friends, announced that he had finally broken off diplomatic relations with a girl-friend of long standing. Returning from her suburban front room one night for the last time, he had come laden with the bric-à-brac of such affairs, arrived at Charing Cross Station depressed by their weight and their romantic connotations and, rather than continue his journey with them, had dumped them at the Left Luggage office, where, for all he cared, they could moulder till the end of the world.

Always prepared to make efforts to improve my musical outlook, Klein on this summer afternoon thrust the Left Luggage ticket in my hand, advising me that if I cared to take the trouble, I would find among the debris of his late love affair four Ellington sides which would do my musical soul the world of good. In the end, determined that I should not duck out of an improving experience, as was my tendency then and since, he accompanied me to Charing Cross himself, where, at the Left Luggage counter, under the glazed eye of a cunning uniformed effigy of a railway porter, we rummaged among the relics, and from the gallimaufry of souvenirs of Cuba, toilet bags, dog-eared paperbacks, post-cards from scattered watering-places, a table-lamp and an ocarina, we found four sides by the Ellington band which Klein ceremoniously handed over with the advice that I should spend enough time with them to convince myself of their merits, taking care to remind me that it was me that was on trial and not the music. As one of the four sides happened to be 'I Got It Bad and That Ain't Good', my conversion was effected almost before it began.

There were three features of that masterpiece which bowled me over. One was the soprano playing of Johnny Hodges which, although I had been acquainted with it for many years already, never failed to overawe me. The second point was the beautiful economy with which Ellington, or perhaps Billy Strayhorn, had compressed the unusually wide leap of the interval of a major ninth which occurs in the first bar of the melody, simply by dropping the higher note by an octave, and making the resultant phrase part of a sequence spreading over the first two bars of the last eight of the last chorus. This paraphrase was played in unison, fanning out into harmony after a dramatic though muted sforzando at the beginning of the third bar, the whole section being so finely conceived and so meticulously executed as to leave no doubt of the originality of the mind which had conceived it. There was a third point which interested me for rather different reasons. The vocal was sung by Ivie Anderson, whose elfin voice and personality had made an impression on me which had lain forgotten somewhere at the back of my mind ever since my first attendance, some time in the mid-1940s, at a performance of 'A Day at the Races'. In the famous stable sequence of that film she had sung 'All God's Chillun Got Rhythm' with the kind of style and sense of irrepressible joy which Hollywood usually managed to suppress with such ruthless efficiency. Away from the vo-de-o-do of that scene and the distracting genius of Groucho Marx, she was suddenly revealed to me as a unique jazz singer.

From this moment of discovery, the vast corpus of Ellington's recorded music became a continent to be charted, a task whose enormity has been complicated by the fact that Ellington has never stopped adding to it ever since. He was born in the reign of Queen Victoria, during the McKinley administration, a few months before Armstrong, and as the years of my jazz life have raced by, the fear that either or both of these men might soon die has haunted the consciousness of almost every musician of my acquaintance articulate enough to discuss jazz at all. There was a feeling among my generation that if and when those catastrophes occurred, then jazz itself would be permanently diminished.

The only words Armstrong ever addressed to me were 'I'm sure glad to meet you English cats', but Ellington I did come to know a little better. I was once hired by a television company to write a script for him, which was of course impossible for me and insulting to Ellington, as anyone but a television company would have known, and when I explained my difficulty to him, he advised me to collect my cheque while he spoke his own words, which he did, talking sweetly throughout a programme whose producer had had the interesting idea that everything would sound much better if Johnny Hodges blew his solo in 'Mood Indigo' perched on a podium of unspeakable vulgarity twenty-five feet above the rest of the orchestra. There was also a night once, after a London concert, when Ellington sat in his hotel drawing-room and did one of his party pieces, recalling his early days as a bandleader in and around his home town of Washington during the First World War. The talk was so intriguing that even as I was enjoying it I made a resolution to memorise it and write it all down. And I did memorise it; unfortunately I delayed the writing down until in time the recollection of everything that had been said began to blur, until now, ten years later, there remains only the recollection of Ellington's smiling face, and the well-bred effrontery of the British free-loaders phoning down for more whisky; also a curious impression of one of those luxuriant pink clouds which figure so prominently in Ellington's programme notes, and which one day will itself evaporate just as surely as the conversation has.

DUKE 1968

Duke Ellington continues to defy credulity. One or two of the musicians with him on the current British tour may differ facially from those who came last year, but the ensemble sound is identical.

As this consistency of timbre never seems to be disturbed by drastic personnel changes, not even the departure of two trumpeters as gifted as Ray Nance and Clark Terry, and as Ellington is the only jazz writer ever to have achieved this blending of other people's personalities into the contours of his own, it seems impossible that the whole thing is luck. Ellington's methods must have something to do with it.

Certainly he composes for individual musicians with profound insight, elegies for Johnny Hodges, snatches of primitivism for Cootie Williams, bland romanticism for Lawrence Brown, dazzling soap-box oratory for Paul Gonsalves. Certainly also he is by now so consummate a master of orchestration that there seems to be no mood he cannot evoke, either with two or three voices or the concerted sound of the fourteen fortunate men working for him.

Of his music on this tour there is nothing new to say. It is either tender or exciting, and always beautiful. But what is the force which has impelled Ellington for forty-three years as a composer leader? No jazz figure has ever baffled so many commentators, including, I suspect, himself. He disarms even the most stringent cross-examination with pink clouds of whimsy. Of attempts to analyse his work he says that 'such talk stinks up the place'. And yet he has also said that 'the memory of things past is important to a jazz musician'.

Most of his newer pieces are offered as impressionistic recollections of places seen and people loved, although there is sometimes the feeling that the programming has been done after the composition has been completed. The point is probably irrelevant. Whatever the inspiration, Ellington manages to go on producing music of importance, and what is most remarkable of all, producing it within a context showing all the signs of decay.

Seen in retrospect, his career has been a triumph of colossal proportions. Ever since he formed a five-piece band in 1923 he has quietly evaded the problems of evolving styles in jazz, choosing instead to find his own way. Sometimes that way has appeared superficially to have been the conventional way, at others to have perilously ignored what seemed to be the only road ahead. And yet today, when jazz seems in danger of disintegration, Ellington alone survives the wreck.

The evidence is all there in the recordings. *The Ellington Era, 1927–40, Volume Two,* contained the clue. Of its forty-seven compositions, thirty-nine are Ellington's, and the advance in sophistication over the period is staggering. None of his works is static. The definitive version is always pursued but never reached, because Ellington himself continues to elaborate even his earliest ideas. And just in case anybody thinks that to make his effects he requires ever-larger orchestras, what of 'Things Ain't What They Used to Be'? Here the ensemble is reduced to eight voices, and no orchestrator could ever have used sparser resources to create such felicitous effects.

In the face of this evidence, Ellington's distaste for analysis is doubly peculiar because there is no musician of this century whose work cries out so much for detailed study, and none more likely to survive it. Tonight at the Albert Hall Ellington joins forces with the London Philharmonic Orchestra, ostensibly to entertain his followers, but in fact to discover a little more about where his limitations might lie. So far the question is unanswered.

1967

When Duke Ellington first recorded his series of Shakespearian vignettes, *Such Sweet Thunder,* there was a general feeling that he had tried to pull a cultural fast one, and that the connection between his music and the characters on which they were supposed to be based was tenuous to the point of nothingness. That was ten years ago, and because the album was deleted from the British catalogues with an indecent haste, the point has hardly been raised since, especially as Ellington himself appeared long ago to have lost interest in the work and no longer presents extracts from it on his concert tours.

The reissue of 'Such Sweet Thunder', therefore, is sure to rank as one of the most interesting events of the jazz year, especially as it seems much clearer now than it did ten years ago that in using Shakespeare as a basis for a series of jazz situations, Ellington created one of his masterpieces.

Not that all suspicions are allayed. There must be some-thing seriously wrong with a portrait of the Shrew which makes her sound like one of Ellington's long succession of innocuous dream-ladies, while Iago seems such a sympathetic chap that one suspects that perhaps he has been confused in the composer's mind with Othello. But for the rest, Elling-ton hits remarkably close to his target without once crippling the jazz potential of his musicians.

Yet the most brilliant successes in 'Such Sweet Thunder' are the sketches of Juliet and Cleopatra, the more so since Ellington, in describing the two poles of womanhood, has used the same musician on the same instrument, Johnny Hodge on the alto saxophone. 'Star Crossed Lovers' is one of Ellington's richest melodies, and evidently Hodges was held close to its written line.

On the other hand, in 'Half the Fun', a witty evocation of Cleopatra's barge sailing down the Nile, Hodges was simply advised to improvise for all he was worth, which was a sensible thing to do, since Hodges's jazz style is as passionate as anything the Queen of Egypt could have mustered.

After ten years it all sounds more impressive than ever, and is probably the only jazz suite by anybody which does not fall between two stools in its attempt to straddle two worlds.

THE DUKE 1969

This year Edward Kennedy Ellington celebrated his seven-tieth birthday, and predictably everybody celebrated with him: radio and television tributes, testimonials from other composers and musicians, even a reception at the White House, where his uncle and father were once employed as butlers.

While Ellington accepts the honours with his characteristic smile of ducal modesty, the jazz world scratches its head and ponders yet again the enigma of its indisputably greatest figure, the man who typifies more than any other the evolv-ing art of jazz and yet outrages all the sacred cows of jazz convention, even to the extent of not accepting the jazz pigeonhole.

Jazz is supposed to be above all an improvised music, yet Ellington has committed it to manuscript and outdistanced all rivals. Jazzmen are supposed to live by a code of integrity so narrow that the outside world is hardly acknowledged at all, yet Ellington will bring to a performance of 'Mood Indigo' or 'Who's Afraid of the Big Bad Wolf?' the same smile of self-absorption.

Leading a large jazz orchestra is so arduous a task and so desperate a gamble that nobody succeeds at it without deploying the tactic of the iron fist in the iron glove, yet in the Ellington band discipline in the conventional sense is so lax as to be virtually non-existent. 'At one time, when we were at the Cotton Club, around 1927, we did have this system of fines and things. But then, you see, Arthur Whetsol was with us. One look from Whetsol . . . everybody started getting into line. We don't have that kind of thing in the present band. It takes too much energy.'

Whetsol, a trumpeter whose work can be heard on many recordings from the early 'jungle' period of Ellington's bewildering development, was one of the very few musicians who joined the band and was not content to spend the rest of his days there. Whetsol left in 1936 to study medicine, but on the other hand a recent discography showed that thirty-one important musicians who have been Ellingtonians averaged sixteen years each in the band. Harry Carney, the band's present baritone saxophonist, has been sitting in the same orchestra chair for the last forty-three years. When asked to explain this very unusual kind of mutual loyalty, Ellington sidestepped the issues with his customary agility and answered, 'I guess Carney will stay for as long as he can afford me.'

Ellington's musical career began in his home town of Washington DC during the First World War, in one of those rare interludes when for a moment the demand for dance band musicians exceeded the supply. 'I put an advertisement in the telephone book bigger than anyone else's. Whenever anybody wanted anything in Washington, they looked in the telephone directory. If somebody wanted to hire some music and didn't know what musicians they wanted, I figured they were just as likely to pick on the biggest advertisement in the book. My hunch worked out pretty well, and before long I had about three bands working.'

Ellington is full of detailed reminiscences of this kind. He was once quoted as saying that the memory of things past is important to a jazz musician, and certainly his own past has made a deep impression on him. Probably for Ellington the best-loved period of all is New York in the early 1920s: work was scarce, but there were heroes to worship and experience waiting to be picked up on every street corner.

It is in the New York of the 1920s, that great time and place of the solo piano masters, that Ellington's own instrumental origins can be found, in the striding right hands and thumping cross-rhythms of James P. Johnson, Willie The Lion Smith and Thomas 'Fats' Waller. Ellington describes these men as his university, and although it is a long time since he amended their Stride piano style to his own ends, to this day the influence of Johnson and Waller can be discerned in his playing, although he is always quick to insist that he was never in their class.

In the past the jazz world has tended to take him too literally on this point and to have underrated him as a piano soloist, for he is an outstanding technician of unmatched harmonic subtlety. It is his lack of pretension about himself rather than any technical weakness which has caused him to be regarded more as a composer-bandleader who happens to play the piano.

His first band had five musicians, including himself, and for some time its members were too preoccupied with finding work to bother very much about changing the course of jazz history. He remembers how he recruited his drummer Sonny Greer in 1923. 'We decided to give him the works and see just what sort of guy he was. We stood on the street corner and waited for him. Everybody used to stand on street corners then and try to look big-time. Here comes Sonny. "Whatcha say" we all ask him. I take the lead in the conversation because I'm sure that I'm a killer with my new shepherd plaid suit, bought on time. Sonny comes back with a line of jive that lays us low. We decide he's O.K.' Greer stayed with Ellington for the next twenty-eight years.

Not until the episode of the Cotton Club in 1927 does Ellington's dossier begin to link with jazz history. By now the band had more than doubled in size and was recording prolifically, mostly Ellington themes composed in the small hours.

His appetite for work was enormous, then as always, and his touching *naïveté* about the mechanics of the musical life was beginning to give way to the extreme sophistication of later years. No longer was it possible for him to try selling a song to a publisher without first equipping himself with a written copy of the work, or to get trapped by circumstances as he did soon after arriving in the big city. 'I was in New York a week and the man came to see me and says, "You're not working tonight, we got to write a show." So I'm stupid, I don't know any different. I says, "Really? Yeah, good", you know. So that night we wrote the show. "Chocolate Kiddies" with Adelaide Hall. It went to Berlin, played two years and the guy who took it there came back a millionaire.'

After the Cotton Club, Ellington's music evolved steadily, until by around 1934 his orchestral textures had moved far beyond the jungle period to a rich impressionism. The original 1937 recording of 'Caravan' is so cunningly wrought that it is impossible to define the moments when the melody disappears and re-emerges on the tide of the harmony. Many connoisseurs feel this was Ellington's golden period, with the 1938–42 band, billed as 'Duke Ellington and his Famous Orchestra', running it a close second. But Ellington refuses to be drawn, and understandably finds the weight of past achievements distinctly oppressive. 'You see, I'm competing against myself. First the 1920s, then the 1930s, the 1940s, the 1950s. Each time it gets a little tougher.'

In a jazz world filled with experts trying to trace the rising curve of his career, Ellington himself looks back only to reminisce, not to analyse. The newest project is the most important one, whether it is a major suite or a four-minute trifle for the dancers.

Most disheartening of all for the musicologists is the virtual impossibility of engaging Ellington in any extended discussion of his methods. But even he must know that there have been great peaks of achievement in his life: 'Black, Brown and Beige' in 1943, his first extended concert work, and the one that finally gave the lie to Constant Lambert's famous appraisal of him as a *petit maître*; the Liberian Suite, the incidental music to 'Timon of Athens'; the series of Shakespearian vignettes, 'Such Sweet Thunder'; the sacred music of the 1960s. Also many band performances of standard jazz themes never since surpassed, either by Ellington or anybody else.

But with Ellington it is very difficult to know. No major artist of this century has a more profound distaste for analysis of and theorising about his work, even though it is more strongly qualified than most to stand such a scrutiny. And to forestall such discussions, he has cultivated that other side of his personality for which he has become world-famous, the bon-vivant who accepts the lionising with graceful good humour. The role is easy for him because he happens to have a most extraordinary gift for courtly behaviour: this would appear quite ridiculous in anyone else, but in Ellington it can charm the birds from the trees.

Most remarkable of all is his effect on women. So far as they are concerned, Ellington once seen is never forgotten. Like Disraeli he believes in laying on the flattery with a trowel. A man escorting a lady off the premises will be gently admonished, 'Never take beauty from a room'. A perfect stranger will be asked, 'Tell me, do you always look as beautiful as this?' A lady who once complimented him on the cut of his jacket was flattened by the response, 'Yes, I was up all afternoon sitting at the loom, weaving it to impress you. It is all an elaborate joke which offends none of the men, rejuvenates all the women and observes one of his golden rules, to make people feel good.'

And yet the deeper one digs under the public persona the more serious a man one discovers. Behind the accomplished social diplomat is a dedicated musician who runs an orchestra for the most hardheaded of reasons. 'I don't want to have to wait around for somebody else to play my music. When I write something I want to hear it now, tomorrow.'

And behind the musician is a deeply religious man whose sacred music bulks largest of all in his mind. 'The sacred concerts are to me the most important thing of all, because they do not constitute part of my career. We don't do it for profit. We play for some churches who have a lot of money, we play for some who don't have any money at all. And whether we win or lose it doesn't make any difference.' Yet on stage nobody cuts a more worldly appearance.

He is, in fact, the sum of many contradictions, a jazz artist who knows that the definition is misleading, if only because music is music and only the unmusical insist on pigeonholes. He is an intensely romantic artist with a superlative shrewdness in dealing with the harsh practicalities of his profession, a generous praiser of other people's work who has never been influenced in the slightest by the shifting tides of fashion in the jazz world, a conjurer who has always insisted there is nothing up his sleeve, and has exasperated the cleverest musicians by the elusive quality of his work. André Previn voiced the bafflement of thousands when he said, 'Stan Kenton can stand in front of a thousand fiddles and a thousand brass and make a dramatic gesture and every studio arranger can nod his head and say, "Oh, yes, that's done like this". But Duke lifts his finger, three horns make a sound, and I don't know what it is.'

Part of the secret lies in Ellington's discovery that the way to write for a group of individuals is to acknowledge their individuality. While every other composer alive writes for instruments, he writes for specific men, so that an unadorned C Major chord can be made to wear a dozen different personalities, depending on the human permutations involved in producing it. For this reason Ellington's music is inimitable.

It is also the reason why he never gets rid of anybody. A new musician is a new texture to be assimilated into the master sound. Yet even here there is a contradiction. Much of his own music can stand without him. Some of his songs (he ranks with Porter, Rodgers and the rest of them as a songwriter) are completely performer-proof.

The biggest irony of all, is that his most famous composition, 'Take the "A" Train', was not written by him at all, but by his beloved partner Billy Strayhorn, who died in 1967.

Broadway's failure to use Ellington's talent ranks as one of the gross musical blunders of our era. An even grosser one is the attitude of the musical world at large, which has usually regarded him as a clever jazz trickster, not much more. Posterity will no doubt reach its own conclusions, and may well decide that he is one of the few authentic melodic stylists of the twentieth century.

But then, as Duke would say, such talk stinks up the place. And, whatever posterity might think of him, he never thinks about posterity at all. He is far too preoccupied with the cut of his clothes, the pattern of his diet, the contentment of his musicians and audiences, his next project, the itinerary for the next tour. Jazz, he once said, is a parade of individuals. Ellington continues to lead the parade.

LOUIS 1963

If there really is anything unique about jazz, it is the ferocious pace of its evolution, from the delicate bloom of its ignorance fifty years ago to its current scrambled pursuit of the techniques of the conservatoire. It has all happened so quickly that it is still possible, in the era of Miles Davis and John Lewis, to witness the performances of Louis Armstrong, a musician whose formative years are inextricably tangled up with the distant legend of the New Orleans heyday.

Armstrong, currently conducting the third British tour of his All-Stars, is now in his sixties, and at least partially inhibited, it would seem, by the aftermath of last year's heart attack. His programme panders quite frankly to that popular market which discovered him, belatedly, about twenty-five years ago, and yet beneath the dross lies a certain incorruptible residue of jazz that will no doubt stay with its owner till his death.

The object-lesson of Armstrong's performances is that jazz music does not rely for its eloquence on tortuous harmonic ingenuities, that it remains a music of personal nuance and inflection, of purely individual interpretation. Whether singing or playing the trumpet, Armstrong bends a note here, syncopates a phrase there, recasts a melody in the shape of the most elementary arpeggios, weaving a spell so potent that it can disarm criticism completely.

To pretend he is still the colossus of the old days would be an insult to some of the greatest jazz performances ever recorded, but even now he is capable of that sudden flash of insight reminiscent of his old mastery. He has been written off so many times that it would be foolhardy to do so again. As recently as 1956 he recorded one of his finest albums, and those who may be disappointed by his choice of material will do well to remember that Armstrong in the studio is a different proposition from Armstrong on the concert stage.

The rest of the All-Stars are in a far less enviable position. Little more than stooges for their leader's whims, their playing rarely rises above the mediocre, with the sole exception of pianist Billy Kyle, who succeeds in remaining smilingly aloof from the dated vulgarities going on around him. Kyle alone plays as though this were a musical recital instead of a knockabout variety act, and produces that fire in the right hand which is one of the glories of the old Earl Hines piano style.

The final testimony to Armstrong's stage craft is to be found in the faces of those leaving the auditorium. If the audience leaves a Miles Davis concert with a distant look in its eye, and a John Lewis recital on tiptoe, it departs from an evening with Louis Armstrong with a broad smile and the happiest of dispositions, like a small boy after watching a Western, which is logical enough.

For Armstrong is the embodiment and the propagator-in-chief of a myth just as potent as the myth of the prairie. His is the myth of the bayou, where the plunking of banjoes under a water-melon moon accompanies the saga of mammies and piccaninnies. The expression of this myth is often trite to the point of imbecility, but Armstrong's apparent belief in its depth renders it somehow moving. He opens and closes his concerts with 'When It's Sleepy Time Down South', a song he has recorded several times. The 'South' referred to is, of course, an imaginary South that never existed outside the swampy terrain of the professional lyric writer, but the melody is well-shaped and beguiling.

Armstrong, croaking away like a retired bullfrog, manages to evoke a mood which sounds like the very soul of jazz. And that is exactly what it is.

LOUIS 1968

The gulf that divides Louisiana from Yorkshire is vast, and as it has taken Louis Armstrong sixty-eight years to span the distance, nobody should be surprised that he has finally arrived at Batley with the fires of his genius burning very low. Armstrong is currently appearing with his All Stars in what looks like the biggest saloon bar in the world, and few of the 2,000 people who are flocking to see him every night have the remotest idea what they are witnessing.

To most of them he is simply the benign old gentleman who persists from time to time in breaking the stranglehold of the younger generation on the Top Twenty. The misconception is understandable. These days Armstrong plays very little trumpet, and no doubt on the advice of his doctors has decided to present himself as a singer instead.

This is the development that the whole jazz world has been dreading for twenty years, the moment of dissolution for Armstrong's heroic trumpet style. So long as he remained young in spirit, then jazz itself could continue to lie about its age, because for so many people the words jazz and Armstrong long ago became synonymous.

But Armstrong plays the one instrument which demands physical strength as well as musical control. The grand old men of jazz, the Bechets and the Ellingtons, might never have lasted so long had they been trumpeters, and even Armstrong the giant who more or less invented the idea of the virtuoso soloist, could hardly have been expected to find a way to preserve the magnificent contours of his instrumental style.

And yet, to those who have the clue, the evidence at Batley suggests that this is precisely what he has managed to do, simply by transferring his genius for improvisation from the trumpet to the human voice. In every bar that Armstrong sings, from the banalities of 'What a Wonderful World' to the authentic jazz overtones of 'When It's Sleepy Time Down South', there is copious evidence of jazz mastery. He has always been an instrumental singer in the sense that the meaning of the words is subordinated to the shapes of the phrases, and if anybody today was to take the trouble to transcribe his vocals on to a trumpet, they would find themselves looking at perfect examples of the art of musical paraphrase.

Not one of his contemporaries from the old days remains a force, and he stands now as the only surviving representative of the emergent days of jazz music. His concerts in London next month will no doubt be well attended for sentimental reasons, but it would be an error of judgement to assume that sentiment will be all. Armstrong, the singer, still retains the power to resolve the complexities of a very elusive art into a sublime simplicity.

LOUIS 1970

For sheer power to excite, no popular artist of this century has remotely approached Louis Daniel Armstrong, trumpet virtuoso and singer extraordinary, who celebrates his seventieth birthday today. His name has only to be mentioned for people to smile in recollection of something they once saw or heard him do.

And yet, as the tributes and the telegrams pour in, the affection of the jazz world at large will surely be tinged with certain pangs of uneasiness, almost as though it were the music itself and not just its most renowned practitioner who was moving into the dangerous age. For ever since he came out of New Orleans nearly fifty years ago, a chubby young man bursting out of a single-breasted dinner suit, to take his music to the cities of the north. Armstrong has been accepted the world over as the physical embodiment of jazz.

He has always managed to look the part without even trying. The staring banjo eyes, the rivers of honest sweat dabbed away by a whiter-than-white handkerchief, the slack lower jaw which has given him the nickname of 'Satch' (satchel-mouth), the illusion of row upon row of sparkling white teeth, the fixed smile and the alarming gravel voice which can somehow make even the most excruciating jive-talk seem witty – all these trademarks, already a little larger than life, have become magnified on cinema screens to be accepted by the average citizen as an accurate representation of what jazz looks like.

Armstrong contrived to preserve this essentially youthful image of himself far longer than anyone could reasonably have expected. Long after most of his New Orleans contemporaries were either dead, or forgotten, or both, and at a stage in life when most people are looking for the nearest armchair, he continued to stick to the kind of working itinerary that would kill a horse. It did seem at times as though his managers were pushing him too hard, or, as somebody recently put it, 'They'd have booked the old man eight days a week if they could.' But the victim appears to have enjoyed every minute of it. Although his life resolved itself many years ago into a crazy dash in and out of aeroplanes, from night club to sound stage to concert hall to recording studio, almost never did his music show signs of fatigue.

Not until very recently did the image begin to fall apart. In the early 1960s came the two heart attacks which have halved Armstrong's effectiveness as a trumpeter, and which have given rise ever since to rumours that he is dead or about to die. Even more drastic have been the effects of his morbid curiosity about the behaviour of his own bowels. This obsession with laxative processes, which began as a joke, has now developed into a mania, reducing the chuckling cherub of the vintage years into a nine-stone wraith whose features can appear shockingly unfamiliar. Customers at his last British season, at Batley in 1968, were dismayed to find that the handout photographs showed a keyhole through which the great man could be seen smiling from his vantage point on a lavatory seat.

It is very doubtful if Armstrong can ever work at full throttle again. His lips, or 'chops', as he has always affectionately called them, can no longer stand the strain of those high notes scattered around with such liberality over the past fifty years. Not that he has lost his grasp of the idiom. An understanding of the nature of music which runs as deep as Armstrong's can never really be damaged. It is simply that physical decline has forced him to accept the fact that if he does play again, it can only be in short, calculated bursts. Not even the bookers who would be pleased to see him perform purely as a singer are able to tempt him out of semi-retirement. Only days ago he was offered 10,000 dollars a night for as many nights as he cared to stipulate, just to sing. But the offer was declined.

Armstrong turns has back on this kind of proposition, not just because he is too tired to accept it, but also because he can afford to indulge the luxury of saying no. There has always been a great deal of uncertainty inside the jazz world as to exactly how rich he is. Probably not as rich as he should be. But although he and those connected with him have always kept the cards very close to their chests in this respect, it is safe to say that he has not had to worry about how much he earns for at least the last twenty years. Perhaps he never did worry too much. To play jazz has always been his way of enjoying himself, a fact which explains much about the effect his performances have. There is even a sense in which he might be said literally to have invented jazz single-handed.

Armstrong the musician is impossible to explain away in purely technical terms. Raised in New Orleans in wretched poverty, at a time when that city was throbbing with the rhythm of the new music, he not only possessed every talent required to master it, but was denied the chance to acquire any talents which might have got in his way. It is important to remember that Armstrong, like so many of his race and generation, is a self-taught musician, not from choice but from necessity.

Ironically, the social prejudices which barred his way to formal training only had the effect of increasing the depth and power of his originality, so that he was obliged to make up the rules of improvisation as he went along, and to break those rules whenever his instincts told him it was right to do so. To this day he is not much of a sight-reader of music, and he recalls his home town less in terms of studies completed than of life lived riotously, and perilously close to the bone.

His love affair with New Orleans, and particularly with its notorious red-light district of Storyville, is probably the most overworked piece of background information in jazz history, not least because 'Satch' himself retains an unquenchable affection for the good old days which keep spilling out in conversation:

Ever since I was a little boy selling newspapers, my mother and father – when they were living together – would tell me lots about Storyville, to kind of frighten me from spending my newspaper nickels down there.

It was just as well for jazz that the advice was ignored, because the Storyville joints were the nearest thing to a university campus he was ever to enjoy.

In any case, New Orleans at that time was so crammed with casual vice, with jazz as its incidental music, that it would have been impossible for any small boy to have avoided it:

I would delight in delivering an order of coal to the prostitute who used to hustle her crib right next to Pete Lala's cabaret, just so I could hear King Oliver play. I'd just stand there in that lady's crib listening to Oliver. All of a sudden it would dawn on her that I was still in her crib very silent while she hustled those tricks, and she'd say, 'What's the matter with you boy?'

And yet Armstrong, who still remembers the layout of the streets and the nickname of every madam, parts company with many of his idolators in his refusal to sentimentalise the music. One of the most surprising and unSatchlike remarks he ever made was, 'You get cliques in a band. Want to play this way and that way, full of that New Orleans fogeyism.'

That remark alone is telling enough to suggest that there is something more to Armstrong than the childlike buffoon with the trumpet. But he once told a few of us something even more revealing, something which actually hints at deviousness and diplomatic shrewdness. He was explaining the astounding fact that for many years he has not been responsible for the choice of musicians who work for him. It has always been assumed that this is merely one more example of his Uncle Tom passivity in the face of overbearing managers. Not a bit of it. 'I never pick my own bands,' he said. 'There are too many good musicians around, and it makes bad friends.'

The Uncle Tom issue has, inevitably, bulked much larger in the past few years, and one has only to examine the sentiments of an Armstrong hit like 'Wonderful World' to see why. He has been accused of selling out to the white commercialisers, of having become a kind of one-man Black and

White Minstrel show, of embracing the old White-Man-Boss relationship with a willingness which says nothing for pride of race or awareness of his own special responsibilities as a figurehead. If the other popular musical figure born on Independence Day, George M. Cohan, is seen as the musical embodiment of Uncle Sam, then Armstrong is just as surely the musical embodiment of Uncle Tom. Or so his detractors say.

They regard him as an old buffer with no relevance to the contemporary scene, and whose popularity is built on the acceptability to the white exploiters of the red-beans-and-rice ethos he has marketed so consistently. They cannot understand why so rich and so gifted a musician should fool about singing 'Hello Dolly' with Barbra Streisand, how he can mouth the lyrics of 'Wonderful World' without baulking at the incongruities.

The interesting thing is that the complaints have all come either from purist critics or political rebels. There is not one single musician of any consequence who takes exception to the personality Armstrong projects on stage, and for a very good reason. It takes a performer to know a performer, and musicians have grasped an obvious truth that the commentators have overlooked, which is that Armstrong's stage life is as much a performance, the projection of an artistic image as any actor's.

He may sing in public of an idyllic Deep South where the banjoes are forever strumming, but the words are no more than musical cyphers to fill up the bars. If Armstrong were really marketing the myth implicit in a song like 'When It's Sleepy Time Down South', he would hardly have sent a bitter telegram to President Eisenhower, as he did when the latter was dealing in his own sweet way with the schools desegregation issue at the time of Little Rock.

Armstrong has not been walking around for fifty years with his eyes closed. He knows all too well what the colour bar has cost him, in the 1930s for instance, when the ballroom bonanza was the exclusive preserve of the white orchestras, or in Hollywood, where he has played a long succession of grooms and valets to a string of leading men who were not fit to wipe his boots, musically speaking. In 1927 he led the first desegregated jazz group to make a record, but he must have noticed that reciprocal gestures from white musicians have not been as frequent as they might have been.

The musicians can't fault him, either on grounds of Uncle Tomism or of anything else, simply because of his infallible professionalism. The respect he commands from fellow-professionals is without equal in the world today and this is because he has been able to do naturally what others have strained to do without ever matching him. It is always forgotten that, in spite of his magnificent legacy of recorded jazz, Armstrong has not for many years been able to make a record in the accepted sense. Nobody is able to book him for a specified number of hours to cut a specified number of sides. His touring commitments have meant that recordings are something achieved on the march, in the middle of the night, piecemeal, between planes and hotels. Had it not been for his freakish stamina and his sense of obligation, Armstrong would hardly have made any long-playing albums at all.

Satch's sessions are like no others. Although not nearly so sophisticated an operator as the moderns, he can pick up an orchestral routine in quicker time than it takes to rehearse it. In fact there are virtually no rehearsals at all. 'It would be a waste of time,' says one man who has recorded him many times. 'You give him the song copy or the lead-sheet, he asks you what you want him to do and then he does it, straight off.' Hardly ever is a second 'take' necessary. He is, in other words, the recording executive's dream, a man who can defy fatigue to produce high quality work in the fastest possible time.

There is even a sense in which Armstrong has been too professional. So completely does he regard himself as an entertainer, and so comprehensive are his gifts, that he will put on record whatever is asked of him, even if it happens not to be worthy of his talents. There is a story about him which is so mawkish that the only excuse for repeating it is that it is quite true. He had come to the end of a particularly gruelling day, ending up in the small hours in a recording studio. The session was over and the musicians packing their instruments. It was then discovered the projected album was one side short.

Armstrong, already heading for the exit, was asked when he could come back to cut one more track. His reply was 'Now.' He sat in a chair and studied the song copy of an old Irving Berlin standard that he had never played before. Would everyone mind waiting just two minutes while he learned the song? Before the two minutes were up he had fallen asleep and tumbled out of his chair, the music still in his hand.

But it would be wrong to see him as a hero martyring himself for the cause. His good humour is irrepressible, and when things go wrong he laughs his way out of trouble, refusing to be pompous about either his own music or anyone else's. When he came to London to appear with a symphony orchestra at a charity concert for the victims of the Hungarian rising, neither rehearsals nor performance went quite according to plan.

At one stage the conductor played the piano while Armstrong ran through one of his routines. At the point where he was to play a four-bar cadenza, Armstrong played eight bars instead. The conductor stopped playing and acidly inquired if Armstrong intended on the night to play a four-bar break or an eight-bar break. Armstrong thought about it for a moment and replied, 'I may do both.' On the night of the concert, orchestral chaos wrecked the performance of one of his favourite spirituals, 'Nobody Knows the Trouble I've Seen, Nobody Knows but Jesus.' Ploughing on through the chaos about him, Armstrong sang, 'Nobody knows the trouble I'm in, nobody knows – but JESUS!'

Basically he is a primitive, an artist with a boldness of approach which has reached heroic proportions. He had no schooling, musical or otherwise, and anyone who can imagine what life was like for a poor black child in the Deep South of sixty years ago must see that it is Armstrong's great triumph to have survived at all. Incapable of intellectualising his part in the evolution of jazz, his rare attempts at critical percipience have usually been disastrous ('These damn be-boppers are killing the business'), while the suggestion that without him, jazz might never have happened at all, would appear to him to be preposterous.

Probably the tributes he prizes most are the ones paid to him by the pioneers of that vanished time and place of his early years. All his rivals loved him in those days, and one of them, a trumpeter called Mutt Carey, said more than all the verdicts of the musicologists put together. When asked what he thought of Armstrong, Carey replied, 'You know it's a pleasure just to hear Louis tune up. Why, just warming up, he blows such a variety of things that it is a wonder to the ears, and a real pleasure.' Carey was right. For more than fifty years, Louis Armstrong has been a wonder to the ears and a real pleasure.

LOUIS 1971

The death last Tuesday of Louis Armstrong two days after his seventy-first birthday was the one death which the jazz world has been dreading for at least the last ten years. There is a very real sense in which this most remarkable man was not only jazz's best known symbol, but the very personification of its spirit. There is, of course, no possibility that any future musician will even remotely approach him: Armstrong's genius was locked into its historical circumstances, both in the sense of his day-to-day life and in the development and maturity of the art form he dominated.

He was born on 4 July 1900 in New Orleans, a time and a place so right for a propagator of this century's most extraordinary musical gospel as to sound like a copywriter's afterthought. But Armstrong really was born in the one town at the one time which made it possible for him to balance the primal joy of his instincts against the high sophistication with which he exploited them artistically. To say he is unique throughout the entire history of art may sound extravagant, but because of the hysterical pace of the evolution of the music he championed, he surely was unique in the sense that he was a primitive who lived long enough to savour the ironies of revivalism, neo-classicism, anarchy, and all the other diversions which art forms so obligingly provide if only we can wait long enough.

The bare facts of Armstrong's life are too familiar to need more than bare mention. Reformatory at twelve, and a chance to learn the trumpet; early musical jobs in the mythical New Orleans of his youth; the summons from his great trumpet hero and father figure, Joe Oliver, to come to Chicago and play second cornet; the move to Fletcher Henderson's orchestra in 1924; the drift into vaudeville, to Broadway, to Hollywood, and the metamorphosis into world figure culminating at the end of his life in a condition so close to fiction that the title song of 'Hello Dolly!' was amended to refer to him.

All this obscures two vital facts about Armstrong the artist, his resilience and his reaction to hardening attitudes in the race war. Behind the chuckling simpleton of popular myth lay a musician who was so resolute a survivor that at the time of his last hit record, 'Wonderful World', many of his old comrades had been dead for thirty or forty years. And the commentators who accused him of exploiting an Uncle Tom image were too imperceptive to see that the great blow Armstrong struck for his race was the mere fact of his existence. By all the odds he should have died in some shack half a lifetime ago, illiterate, unknown, unfulfilled. That he triumphed over the appalling limitations of his environment to become one of the great creative artists of the world is a miracle which posterity will perhaps take less for granted than we do today.

What matters most of all about Armstrong is the residue of music he has left behind. His style had that quality of apparent simplicity which only the complexity of real genius can achieve. Anybody can learn what Armstrong knew about music in a few weeks. Nobody could learn to play like him in a thousand years. Unfortunately, the language of jazz criticism is a currency hopelessly debased by thirty years of hyperbolic lunacy, but Armstrong, with his masculine beauty of tone, his endless inventive resource, his vast instrumental range, demands all the superlatives. The towering, heroic extroversion of his style, shot through with a brio which enabled him to bring jazz to a world which frankly cares very little for it, will prove in time to have been one of the artistic triumphs of the twentieth century.